WHY ME?

A STOLEN CHILDHOOD

Perl LebovitS

ISBN: 978-91-985215-4-2

Table of Contents

Prologue

Thank you, Mom and Dad, for telling me about your experiences. I only wish that you had waited until I was older so I could have better processed your horrible experiences in concentration camps. As it was, I was terrified of the nights and was plagued by nightmares. I remember often looking under the bed to make sure there was no one hiding there who might hurt me. Hearing these things was deeply traumatizing for a small child.

Mom, you started telling me your story when I was four years old. As a four-year-old, I could not process such horrific images, but you told me without a thought of how it would affect me. It was only about how difficult it had been for you. You just assumed I would understand. You put a heavy burden on your baby's shoulders. When I confronted you about this as an adult, you denied it. Why were you ashamed? Was it wise for you to save your soul over your child? How could you be so blunt?

Perhaps it was because you yourself were a child when these horrors happened to you, and you too did not have the opportunity to properly process what happened. But how could you not protect me from the same? For years, I have suffered with your pain. Because of it, I have been exposed to betrayal and mixed goodness with evil. You were not a good role model for me. You weren't there for my emotional needs and put your needs ahead of mine when I was a small child.

You said it was because I was the oldest. Where did that come from? Yes, I was your oldest child, but I was only four years old, and only two and a half years older than your next child. How could that have made sense to you, Mom? Dad worked, and you had no other adults to talk to? You talked to my aunts who took care of their children.

You always compared your parental skills to theirs and thought that they handled their children worse than you. You criticized how one aunt pulled her child's hair and screamed. But you had no insight. You did the same. You screamed, swearing at me in Yiddish. How do you think that made me feel as a little girl?

I was traumatized when you scolded me, and there was no one to protect me from your physical and psychological outbursts. How could you do that? When I confronted you as an adult, you choked me by parasitizing the life energy that I needed for myself, and so it continued. Throughout my childhood, you were a parasite that I wanted to release. I would have chosen another mother who cared about me and my needs, who could have guided me in a balanced way. So many times, I wanted to be adopted. You don't know that, but I really wanted not only a better mother but also a better dad.

If I said anything then you told Dad. I got many slaps from him, and he could get furious and hit me until I fainted and bled profusely from my nose or face. Today I have fibromyalgia, Mother. Where do you think it came from? Blows, cracks, and mental torture from both you and Dad, yes, but unfortunately also from others who continued to do the same things. I was beaten by teachers and students during my schooling and later experienced psychological abuse in workplaces, from friends, and from spouses.

Was it because you wanted me to grow up? The whole time you were jealous that I was growing up in a country without war. But, Mom, it was not my fault that you were involved in a war. I just happened to be born of you. You took all my life energy to cope with life. Shame on you. Sure, I understand that things were horrible for you, but if it was so bad, why did you have children? I did not want such a life. You told me that I was being suffocated during childbirth. I would rather have been suffocated by the umbilical cord than live this life. But, no, Dad made a fuss with a doctor so that you and I both survived.

I might be better off if I let go of this, for my own sake, not for yours. I understand that. But now it's also about my right to a good life, Mom. You always prioritized your needs over mine.

You were a real bull, Mother. You baked, cooked, sewed, knitted, and cleaned. From the outside, you looked like a great mother. You offered neighbors and acquaintances advice, so everyone had something good to say about you. You were able to be kind to strangers but not to me.

Of course, you could switch from hostile one second to a playful mother the next, but it was very difficult to take it in. When you were nice, I liked to be close to you even though you thought I was too clumsy. I would rush to grab my shoes to accompany you when you went shopping, a poor little girl trying to get some love from you when you felt good because the opportunities were few and far between.

And you, Dad, who came home after not having been with us all day, you were tired and just sat in your armchair. As a little child, I brought you slippers like a puppy. You gave me sweets to show your appreciation, and I got too many cavities at an early age. I was treated like a dog that would come when called, wearing fine clothes and with well-brushed hair. I don't have many memories of you, Dad.

Once you told me that I went with you to the Skansen zoo where you taught me how to identify birds. Others were so interested in what you were saying that they followed after us to listen. I do not remember this, but I know enough different bird species, so you may have taught me the birds. I kept the Focus encyclopedia books that I looked at with you. I also remember the One Thousand and One Nights, which I also kept. But most of all, I remember how you beat me when Mom complained about how disobedient I had been. She lied. I tried to tell you when I was older.

When I was a kid, you told me that you were sick and just wanted one child. I was enough for you. But then my mother wanted more children, and you went along with it but couldn't cope with them. You tried to tell me it was Mom who made the decisions at home and that you were addicted to her care.

Did Mom force you to beat me? Or was that your idea? I don't know. I just received blows, kicks, and had hair pulled out of my scalp. You also didn't like being interrupted, and we had to sit on needles for hours to listen to you talk. We never interrupted. If we children did, then you beat us. You even hit me in front of guests. We had a nice guest who often visited us on Friday nights. I served the guest soup. He did not want soup. You intentionally humiliated me.

Was I your house slave? It seemed that way. I had to help with labor-intensive chores like pulling heavy wagons filled with bags of potatoes, onions, and other produce when we went shopping.

I had to carry heavy bags of dirty clothes and wash them in the smelly laundry room. I had to cook with Mom and keep an eye on the meat for hours. I beat the carpets, vacuumed, dusted, scrubbed pans, and cleaned kitchen cabinets and benches. Homework I would struggle through when the household chores were completed. Early on, you said that you could only help with housing, food, and necessary clothing. If I wanted anything else, I would have to start working. I did that too and tried working for a neighbor in a filthy garage with old men who hung smut pictures on the walls. What happened there?

Later, I got a job at the post office for five kronor an hour, which I saved. When I was fourteen, we children would all help by dragging home things you bought like heavy furniture, crystal, and paintings. You thought you were getting a bargain and were happy about it. Without asking, you took the small savings I had in my bank account, and did the same with my siblings' savings, to buy more things.

But I'd kept my pennies at the post office and traveled to Hungary with Mom. It was my first trip abroad. We traveled by train for over a day and a half, heading towards Yugoslavia. It was dirty and crowded, and my mother was afraid at every border station that she would be held. Memories of the war appeared to still be strongly with her. We had barely any money in Hungary and stayed with your cousin who was a real bitch that milked Mom for things like coffee and clothes. She complained that we only had brewed coffee with us. She had wanted Nescafé.

Then you had a plan, Dad, that I would marry a man ten years older, so he could live in Sweden and work as a doctor. I was seventeen years old and thought he was an old man. He wanted five kids with me, and I ran from there. You treated me like an asset. You wanted to sell me so that you would have a doctor in the family, but you didn't get the chance. It was so primitive, just like the Arabic families do with their daughters when they come to Sweden, which disgusts everyone. Yet it was my reality when I grew up in a Jewish family. Why?

Not many of my companions were treated as badly by their parents as I was. Then you had delusions when I wanted to accompany my best friend on vacation. Her dad worked at Scandinavian Airlines, so I would have been able to go with them for free. I would have gladly followed along to get to go to New Jersey and other places. But, no, it did not work out. According to your twisted head, her father might rape me. You thought that about all men. Why?

It was so important to you that I marry an Orthodox Jewish man, so I just married a man like you in the hopes of finding peace and quiet, but he destroyed my life. I say I chose him, but my choices were limited. I did not choose for myself and absolutely not for joy. Then you declared me dead. You had given away my rights as a daughter.

I was terrified of being condemned and left alone. But I was still alone with all the obscurity that came from being married to the man who destroyed my life. This you understood later, but by then it was already too late. When I needed to disengage myself from that relationship, I had a friend whose husband helped me. It took three years. Not even then could you help me. Only when it was over were you glad I was divorced.

Did you want me to live as a divorced woman with an autistic child? Was that your dream for me? Was that why I came as a child to you, Dad? What have you done?

I had to cope with everything myself, for neither Mom nor you managed to accept that my son was autistic. It would go away. Is that what you thought? And what did you do to arrange specialists to help him? As usual, nothing. I have always been an orphan, forced to be my own mother and father. I regret that I did not leave the family. If I had not been your daughter, maybe I would have had a better life.

Despite everything, I have forgiven both Mother and you because of your shortcomings. I have also tried to forgive myself for the scars you caused me, so I can be free. It has taken my whole life, forged by various efforts from all over the world. I hope now in my sixties to find peace, to come out as the person I truly am, and succeed with my gifts to achieve what I really deserve.

Thank you, my son, for daring to become my child even though you struggled with me as a single mother. There was no dad to help you, and your grandparents would take you only when they were happy. Unfortunately, you had no contact with your other grandparents because they were ten times crazier. You had some contact with my siblings when they were able to, and of course, with me.

Then when you grew up, others took care of you, like where you now live. I have tried to help you in every way I can. But I did not choose this. I hope I have been a good mother. I have been pressured to be both a mother and father in all situations. It was not easy. It was particularly difficult on the nights when you could not sleep, and I had to go to work unreasonably early to support us. There was no other option. I spent a lot of time at home with you since the school could not manage the difficulties you had. We have nevertheless done some fun things and traveled a lot both in Sweden and abroad, something I never got to do with my parents. I have tried to give you the best possible living conditions within your disability and to help you find interests.

We have had twenty-five art exhibitions that mean a lot to both you and me. Art is your lifeblood. You are a good artist, and others appreciate it now. Perhaps not as an artist in some circles, but you are well on your way. Your dad was away for over ten years and suddenly appeared when you moved away from home. He claimed that I prevented him from meeting you, which is a lie. When no one wanted to form a family with him, he decided it would be good to come back and try to play daddy to you. Now every week, he calls the day before to check that he can come.

Because he has let you down, you want to avoid many of his gifts. Despite that, he betrays you. He greets you on his terms because he is invited for dinner and coffee. Now I have asked him to pay the costs when he is with you because you do not receive any salary, only habilitation compensation during the days. He doesn't understand better.

I hope you will have as well of a life as possible, but I must also have a better life. You understand I have had to make such big sacrifices, so I have not reached where I want to be. People around you have not always done what we agreed on, so I have had to keep hold of the reins for a very long time and do things you do not understand but need. Otherwise, everything would have completely fallen apart, dear child.

I thank God and all the positive angels who made it possible for my son and me to move on.

Background of the People and Settings

My grandparents on my mom's side lived in Mukachevo with the Munkacs Jewish community. So did my grandparents on my dad's side.

Shreigel is my mom's father, and Perl is my mom's mother. I never met either of them. Aunt Elsa is my mom's aunt. Hersh-Leib is my mom's oldest brother, Shoshi is her third oldest brother, and Abraham is her youngest brother, none of whom I have met. Magda is my mom's sister, and Jölan is her oldest sister. I have met both of them.

Dr. Mengele was a Nazi and a mass murderer. He experimented on people in a monstrous way.

Stürmfuhrer Adolf Eismann a Nazi and a mass murderer.

Magda and Jölan are my aunts.

Magda's son's name is Tommy. I met him. Jölan's son is Bill (fictive name).

Malvina is my moms name.

Ludvig is my dads name

Byk Family – a Jewish orthodox family that helped my parents get married in Stockholm

Klippgatan – a Jewish community houses for concentration camp survivors in Stockholm

Vitabergsparken – the name of a park near to Klippgatan

Kungsträdgården – a park in the middle of the city

EPA – a well-known warehouse

Van der Nootska – a well-known palace in south Stockholm close to the synagogue

Grandmother – my dad's mom, who I never met; she moved to the United States

Grandmother Perl I am named after died at the concentrationcamp with Abraham -my uncle.

Danny – my bother (fictive name)

Vera- my sister (fictive name)

Pelle Svanslös – a well-known cartoon character and also a candy

Getfotsvägen – the street my family lived on from the late fifties to the mid-sixties

Saint Lucia – a Swedish holiday celebration that takes place on December 13

Silva – my first school teacher, an older woman from Germany

Gubbängstorget – a square in Stockholm close to the school I was attending at the time

Helen – one of my chubby friends

Raul Wallenberg – a well-known Swede that helped Jews escape from the Nazis in Budapest; He was deported to Russia.

Södersjukhuset – the hospital where I was born in 1957

Djurgården – a well-known recreation area in the middle of town with a lot of natural areas, amusement parks, museums, and restaurants.

Norrmalmstorg – in the middle of town in Stockholm

Dov Dinur – a professor of history who specialized in the life of concentration camp survivors in Sweden, and a close friend of my dad's from Mukachevo

Anna – fiction name for my best friend in Hillelskolan (the Jewish school)

Jan – Anna's father (fictive name)

Björksätraskolan – a school near where I lived

St. Paul's Street – a street in SoFo in Stockholm

Hökarängen – a fictive name for a suburb

Gunnar – my basketball coach in school (fictive name)

Sten – a classmate (fictive name)

Sara – a classmate (fictive name)

Sarah – a classmate and friend (fictive name)

Zara – a high school classmate who was evil to me (fictive name)

Säbel – a school teacher

Lars – a classmate's fictive name

Alice – a teacher's daughter (fictive name)

Bettan – a classmate and friend (fictive name)

Kent – a classmate from Hillelskolan (fictive name)

Erik - a classmate from Hillelskolan (fictive name)

Marita Pajajusis – my teacher at Hillelskolan

Leif – a classmate at high school (fictive name)

Palmgrenska – co-educational half-private school where some classmates from Hillelskolan went to high school

Whitlockska- co-educational half-private school where I was sewing.

Madame Rochas – a perfume

Harry – a classmate who went to Palmgrenska as well (fictive name)

Avraham Rechelbach – a Hebrew teacher

Miss Uhr – a teacher at Palmgrenska

Mr. Müller – a classmate at Palmgrenska

Urban – a classmate at Plamgrenska (fictive name)

Putte – a classmate from Hillelskolan (fictive name)

Nicklas – fictive name for a classmate at Hillelskolan

Gunnar– a classmate from Hillelskolan (fictive name)

Anders – a man ten years older than me who admired me (fictive name)

Zoltan – a dance teacher (fictive name)

Le Chat – a French soap

Frans Schartaus – a high school gymnasium

Bo- a classmate from Frans Schartaus high school

Iza-My dad's cousin in Budapest

Robbi – my second cousin. Itza's son

Kia – a classmate from Frans Schartau (fictive name)

Bert Zaras – a boyfriend (fictive name)

Jörgen – a classmate at Frans Schartau (fictive name)

Mia – fictive name of a classmate from Frans Schartau

Tor Wertsus, Totte – my main teacher in Frans Schartau

Sune Eklund – a fictive name for a law teacher and coach at Frans Schartau, an evil man

Valborg – a Swedish holiday, April 30

Östermalmstorg – an upper-class area of Stockholm, like Manhattan in New York.

Inger – a twenty-year-older student at the university, very left-oriented

Bill – my cousin (fictive name), Jölan's son.

Malvina – my mom

Ida – a fictive name of a student from the university

Pia – my name

Arvika – a smaller town in northern Sweden

Rådmansgatan – a street in the city of Stockholm

Jay- a man I met in the Golan hights in Israel and later in New York.

Nelly – my dad's cousin in Jerusalem

Jay – a man I dated in New York

Dana – my second cousin in New York (fictive name)

Philip – fictive name of my son

David – fictive name of my ex-husband

Johanna – David's mom

Kurt – fictive name for David's dad

Carina – fictive name for David's cousin

Rabbi Smalts – a fictive name of a rabbi I didn't like

Patch family¬- a fictive name of the family I married in to

Dov Feinstein – a fictive name of a cantor

Stallmästaregården- A place was our wedding settled.

Gunilla – a fictive name for one of my best friends

Tallkrogen at Svanbacken – a fictive address we lived at when David married me.

Philip- a fictive name of my son

Gubbängen a fictive place my parents lived.

Tallkrogen – a fictive suburb

Silbersky – a well-known lawyer

Billner – my lawyer

Rabbi Emil – one of David's grandfathers, a chief rabbi of the fictive city Bologna (fictive name)

Konsum – a food store

Alma – a friend of mine (fictive name)

Sanna- a friend of mine, Married to Bengt (fictive name)

Bengt helped me with the orthodox jewish divorce

Olga – a fictive name for Phillip's preschool teacher

Bengt – husband to a friend of mine (fictive name)

What Mom Told Me

I will start by telling you about how my mother had been before her father died.

My mom's family lived in the then Czech Republic in a town called Munkacs or Mukacevo. Their pink two-story house was in the stone pits that Grandfather owned. Mother lived there with six other siblings. Grandma and Grandfather had a grocery store with a large assortment of merchandise, and they owned properties.

Grandma had gray-green eyes and a common appearance. She always wore a headscarf and long-sleeved dresses. She had a good heart and a great deal of integrity. They helped people who couldn't pay with housing and food. Grandma came from the country. Mom told me that they had to ride a bus for a whole day to get there.

Grandpa had a beautifully open face with soulful, intense blue eyes, a straight nose, and shapely lips. He was a righteous person known for his good heart, a tzaddik. His Jewish first name was Shreigel, and his given name was Stern. His grandparents came from Vienna. Mom looked a lot like him. Mom was the apple of grandfather's eye. She was beautiful as a child with tight curls, big blue-gray eyes, and an open face with beautifully shaped lips. People told her she was as pretty as a gypsy, who were thought to have particularly beautiful children.

They lived in an idyllic small town below the Carpathians with a large Jewish population. I watched videos and looked at pictures of the area so that I could imagine what it might have been like to live there. The scenic area had mountains, lots of coniferous forests, fields, and streams. In the video, I saw men fishing for carp and then taking a dip. Mom thought it was beautiful too, but she probably hadn't seen any fish.

The video showed other views and then a car struggling to drive across the difficult terrain. The street was not paved, and the houses looked dilapidated with gates reminiscent of the yellowing black and white photo I have of Grandpa's house. Could it be where they once lived? I have no idea. I looked at the street names on a map, but the big one I found was in Russian. I can only read a few Cyrillic letters that my dad tried to teach me once. I got annoyed and finally found a map that I could read the names on, but I still couldn't find Kochot Uza. I think the name must have been changed. I saved all the video clips to watch later.

Mom was born in 1929 in Czechoslovakia, as it was then called, where the Jews lived very religiously. They spoke Czech, but Mom learned to speak and write Hungarian. She was the second youngest child and often played with her youngest brother, Abraham.

Jölan was the oldest girl and learned to sew early on. They planned for her to marry young, and she needed to learn a profession to be attractive as a bride because she was not especially beautiful. One of the middle sisters, Magda, got to learn a little too but not as much. One day, a gypsy grabbed her sack and wanted to rob her. She screamed so loudly that a passerby heard and cut the sack to rescue her. I don't know how old my mother was at the time.

I have some photos of the house and the surrounding area where Mother grew up, and it looked like a midsize city. The house had a plastered façade, and there was a backyard with a fence that separated the yard from the street. There were walking paths to a park, and a market where fruits and vegetables were sold by Russian-looking vendors wearing shawls and aprons over their skirts.

The market must have been where Mom bought a big melon that rolled away from her. I think there are watermelons in some of the stands in the black and white photos, which fits with the snippets of what my mother told me.

Grandma and grandfather struggled to run their little grocery store and support seven children. Mom grew up with different aunts and nannies who took care of her. She hardly ever had a chance to talk with her mother.

Grandpa had a brother who was an engineer and drove a car, which was unusual in the late 1920s. He was as handsome as Grandpa with a similar appearance. He was married to a beautiful woman whose mother was named Elsa Ninni, Aunt Elsa.

Mom remembered Aunt Elsa combing her hair, and Mom dared to replicate the same hairstyle. Aunt Elsa kept red lipstick and other makeup in a nightstand. One day, Mom took the opportunity to dress in some fashionable clothes and put on high heels. She had made an extra effort to paint her mouth in red and put blush on her cheeks, trying to change her appearance. Grandma didn't like it, so Mom was reprimanded when Grandma came home. Mom also remembers listening to the radio with Aunt Elsa and talking to her when they drank afternoon tea and ate small cakes.

Mom told me they had a Shabbos goy that kept the house heated and the food hot on Shabbat. They had several boiling vessels in an oven in the courtyard that was kept warm during the Shabbat and festivals. It was Mom's job to make sure that the food was there and that the Shabbos goy understood what was needed.

In 1933 the Hungarians invaded the city. The Hungarian Nazis, called the Arrow Cross Party, were horrible and aligned with the German Nazis.

In the film I watched, I saw a woman spinning. She sat wearing a headscarf and a long-sleeved dress. She spoke Yiddish with the same accent my parents had. The men in the 1930s wore fur hats called *shtreimel* and had payot (sidelocks). Often they wore dark coats.

The film showed a boy who came into a bookstore and bought a book for fifty korun (the currency in the Czech Republic). Small children wearing skirts, blouses, white knee socks, and combed hairstyles stood in a line proudly singing Israel's national anthem. A few years later, most of them were killed. At the end of the video, young people danced in a circle

Mom never returned to her hometown. She was afraid of being harassed by the Russians who had taken her father's house and possessions. Mom said her dad got hit in the head with a brick because he did not participate in transporting people to concentration camps. My grandpa died in mother's arms. Mom was nine years old and didn't really understand what happened. When Grandma realized this, she broke down. War became more and more common.

Older brother Hersh-Leib was responsible for the family and served in the military. By the time he came home, he had contracted typhus. Grandmother cured him with fresh milk and easily digested food. The older sons had to contribute in every way to the family's livelihood. Mom's third brother, Soshi, worked as a peddler. He had a small rolling shop where he sold embroidered handkerchiefs, threads, needles, notepads, pencils, erasers, and other necessities.

Mom told me that as the Hungarians became more and more anti-Semitic, the children could be beaten because they had a little dirt under their nails. Mom helped all her classmates borrow clean napkins from Soshi. When the teachers inspected the children, they would slam their hands with a stick. The children could also get several lashes with a rattan cane while facing the class if they didn't have supplies like notepads, pencils, and erasers.

Despite all these horrible things, in 1939, Mom and Aunt Magda got to perform traditional dances in the Hungarian theater while wearing red leather boots with the typical national costumes. Mother's native language was Czech, and she appreciated being able to represent her heritage even after the Hungarians had invaded the the Czech Republic.

Mom told me about the war and how she rode a crowded train back and forth in cattle cars. She did not fit and had to squeeze between other children and adults with her mother and brother. Mother's brother, Abraham, was thirteen years old. Mother was fourteen, and my Grandmother was forty.

They arrived at a final station, and mom held my Grandma's right hand tightly as they stepped off the train. They saw black-dressed men in mid-length coats roaring in German as they held German shepherds on leashes. Mom often told me how she, her little brother, and Grandmother got off the train at Auschwitz and were forced to stand at different stations where the people were divided into groups based off whether they were elderly, adult, or children. The Germans counted one, two, three, four, five left. One, two, three, four, five right. Five by five were counted from morning through the evening. It was called appeal. This frenetic chaos was the count of the slaves five by five.

I read in a report that it was über sturmführer Adolf Eismann who loaded the Jews from Mukacevo into the wagons and that they traveled for about four days to different places before they ended up in Auschwitz. Über sturmführer Mengele asked the arriving children and young people how old they were. It could happen several times every day.

Mom told me that when she came with her mother and little brother, a Nazi asked her how old she was. Grandma had instructed her to give a younger age so that she could be with the other children. But, like a flash from clear sky, my mother tugged at her cheeks and said she was older instead. Mom said she was seventeen, and Grandmother shook her arm, shouting.

Mom was in shock and ran and ran into the forest.[1][2] See Inanna's journey and the description of the myth for an understanding of the descent into the underworld and all the difficulties she faces. My mother was forced as a child into this descent, unaware what horrors would happen to her during

---

[1] Inna's journey by Sylvia Brinton Perera
[2] Anita Goldman, The Love Course (page 92-94)

the war. She survived, but her phases got stuck. She didn't make it all the way out of the descent. The child was deprived of her innocence and trust. A large piece of my mother's soul died in the concentration camp's descent. She tried to heal by telling me about her trauma, but I was only four years old.

My mother grabbed onto me by telling me about these horrors. She unknowingly tried to get out of the cave of suffering she had been stuck in. In the myth, Inanna is in a chaotic situation filled with fear. For Mom, it was always monstrous and paralyzing, depriving mother of her defense and security.

The Nazi broke her grip from her mother and screamed that she would run from there. Grandma and Uncle were trapped in a queue. Mom wandered around in the chaos, and later in the evening, she caught hold of a woman who told her that Grandma and Mom's little brother were in the smoke that came from the gas chamber.

Mom felt like Inanna in the myth. "In the end, she walks completely naked and bent forward to her sister who hurls the scream of guilt." Descent. "It is Inanna, the queen of the earth and heaven in the ancient Sumer, descending into the underworld, to the great unknown." She must leave all her belongings and go down to the underworld where her sister Ereshkigal lives. She tells her servant woman that, if she does not return, to seek out Father Enki, the god of wisdom. He will save her.

Ereshkigal ensures that Inanna makes her entry into the underworld deeply bent. At every post on the road, she has to take something off, be deprived of something. At the first its shugurra, a crown of the steppe, at the second a small lapis necklace, and at the third a double strand of beads. Every time she protests, she gets the answer: "Quiet Inanna, the ways of the underworld are perfect." Ereshkigal put the eye of death on her. She strikes Inanna, turning her into a piece of rotting meat, and hanging her on a hook in the wall.

Three days and nights elapse, but Inanna does not return. The servant tears his body in grief, goes to one god after another, but everyone responds that the person who is drawn to the Great Ned must blame himself. Everyone except Father Enki, who reacts differently. "I'm worried," he tells the servant[3]. From the dirt under his fingernail, he creates two creatures. To one he gives the food of life and to the other the water of life. He instructs them to go down into the underworld, transforming into flies.

After descending into the world that belongs to Ereshigal, they hear the moans, "Oh, oh, my back. Oh, my heart... Oh, my liver." The two visitors complain to her, repeating her every word. This is what she wants[3], to be heard in her pain. Now she wants to give them a gift as a thank you. But they do not want either the water or the other gifts offered to them. They just want the meat that Inanna has become that hangs from the hook. Inanna's body is handed over to them, and they sprinkle the food and water of life on her. Inanna is resurrected. Enki, the god of wisdom, had saved her[3].

Mom had broken down but ran back that evening and asked if anyone had seen her mother. The experience gave Mom a dark feminine wisdom that she couldn't bear. Mom did not cope with the

---

[3] Anita Goldman, The Love Course (page 92-94)

myth of Psyche where she used the knowledge to make Aphrodite beautiful and eternal "to keep Eros"[4]. When Psyche is to fetch the source, it is a box of insomnia to make her fall asleep in the underworld so that evil Aphrodite can get her hands on Eros. But Eros comes to life and takes Psyche out of the underworld.

Mom was petrified and cold and misguided in what she thought was appropriate to tell me. Mom was not going to wait to tell these terrible things to me when I was older. She lacked the objectivity that would protect me. I needed to make Inanna's descent[5] with my mother. My mother clung to me like a child.

In an essay written for Lund University, "A Study in the Author Sanfrid Neander-Nilsson's View on 'Swedishness,'" I read that Neander-Nilsson studied the Jews in Mukacevo during the 1930s. The name of the city is spelled differently depending on whether it is written in Czech, Hungarian, or Russian. He thought they took over the city and did not consider the Christians. He was angry with how there could be a Jewish mayor in the city and that even the Czech bus system did not drive the bus on the Shabbat (Saturday). He thought the Jews threatened to take over. He had also studied at the Institute of Racial Biology in Uppsala, which conducted research on Jews. They did drawings showing what the Jewish skull and foot look like, implying that Jewish people had an inferior walking style.

The difference between Swedes and Swedish Jews was, according to Neander-Nilsson, that the Swedes always used the earth, and it was natural for them to be in the countryside. The Jews were greedy and engaged in money-making ventures. The Jews from the east were peddlers, and people should beware of them. Sweden strongly supported Nazism between 1930–1945, and the farmers were the true Arians who completely devoted themselves to nature. However, the author wrote that the Swedes were melancholy.

I wonder how much the author and his time in Sweden influenced the Nazi killing of my relatives in Mukacevo.

I became my mother's four-year-old mother. This happened to me against my will. The elder showed my mother a chimney with smoke. "There she is." Mom tells me this like a mantra, with an empty look in her eyes. She didn't want to think my grandmother and uncle were dead. At the time, she had run around looking and finally found her sisters. This stuck with me, and I dreamed as a child that I was involved in some way.

Mom didn't understand what gas chambers were. She was only fourteen years old. After she finally found her sisters, they tried to help each other through the war. Mom was the youngest and most beautiful. She was particularly vulnerable to her oldest and ugly sister who was envious. They were three of them, and Mother was closest to Magda, who was some years older.

I remember when she told me that a newly redeemed mother was forced to watch a Nazis throw her child into the latrine. Her baby suffocated in the feces as the Nazi roared with laughter. Ereshkigal embodies one of the gods' prescribed facts that "death ceases all life" [5], that birth and

[4] Inna's journey by Sylvia Brinton Perera
[5] Inna's journey by Sylvia Brinton Perera

life are intimately associated with a woman's history. She suffers from patient submission but endures. I read further that Dr. Mengele, as he was called, conducted cruel experiments on the Jews from his mother's hometown. He did special experiments with twins. Mom told me about this, but I also read about the various blood transfusions he performed between twins. He would inject mucus into people's hips and various soft tissues so they fell ill and died faster. He also injected people with typhoid and various forms of gases and toxins before they were tortured to death.

Dr. Mengele tortured people without anesthesia. On Jewish festivals such as the Jewish New Year, Rosh Hashanah, and the Day of Atonement, Yom Kippur, he was extra cruel with his torture, especially of children, as a bonus to his tyranny.

Mom did not succumb as a teenager of this failure. She endured but could not move on. The visuals remained with her forever. Mom chose me as her fellow traveler, and then, in a terrible way, I became co-dependent, trying to help her out of the pain. I became Heavenly Aphrodite and Mother became the Underground Aphrodite that Sylvia Brinton Perera depicts in Inanna's journey[6]. The upper part is the caring caregiver while the lower part displays impersonal, aggressive, and passionate energies. My grandmother couldn't help her, so I became a substitute for her. I resisted, as a four-year-old does. I put my hands over my ears and didn't want to listen.

I heard the eyewitnesses who recorded their stories (in Yad Vashem, a center dedicated to the Holocaust of Jews in Jerusalem) who lived in my parents' hometown about how they were trapped in crowded wagons that were for animals. How the worst stench of urine feces burned there nostrils. There was no toilet, and they did not open a window, instead wandering back and forth without knowing what they were supposed to do. Mom also told me about this as a child.

The first place they went was Krakov. Other small towns before Auschwitz played an orchestra that welcomed the prisoners at a sign that read *ARBEIT MACHT FREI*. When they arrived, a woman told them to change into striped pajamas and yelled at the young mothers not to hold their babies, telling them they should leave their children with their grandmothers. They tried to help them by screaming that no one should admit to having a twin. The new arrivals took nothing with them. Very quickly they realized from the warnings that they were to be used in various experiments.

I don't know if Mom saw any of the experiments that were performed on people. She didn't go into detail about that. However, she was terrified of being killed for the smallest thing. She told me how grateful she was for a bread crust and something to warm up with. She gave away her coat when her aunt froze. She thought that God would protect her and that she was doing well because of her youth.

Without warning, Mom's mood would shift, and she would ignore me no matter what I did. She had extreme mood swings, shifting at a moment's notice from being happy to breaking out into total hysteria and anger. She had also told me about the narrow bays in Auschwitz and how they lay there dirty with the lice crawling over them, and that at any time at night, they might have to stand up to be counted, five by five. Inanna is tethered, suspended on the hook. Ereshkigal wails. There is no hope, no way through work or will. This is the goddess's dark side. Mom was like a piece of meat suspended on a hook, left to rot in the underworld.

In a pure panic, Mom tried to take all the straws to save herself and was willing to sacrifice my well-being to do it. Did she ever consider that I might be terrified of these stories? That maybe I thought as a child that a Nazi would wake me up to shoot or torture me? I asked Mom to stop telling me, but she couldn't. She said she told me so I could tell others, but I was just a little girl. Mom didn't care about me. She was as helpless as in the situation she was subjected to, still stuck in the terrible tragedies she'd witnessed.

For me as a small child, it was extremely difficult, the unpredictability of feeling safe one moment then becoming insecure from being forced to grow up as I heard horrors that a small child could not sort. Mom had often asked the Nazis to shoot her when it was too difficult for her to endure what she was living through. They replied that she was not worth a bullet.

Mom struggled through the cold, starvation, and mental and physical torture for a year. She was forced to march for several miles at the end. I don't know for how long. Magda told me that she saved Mom, who fell down several times. Aunt Magda was the one who kept Mom alive. Jölan did better because she was the oldest. Every time Mom was close to giving up, Magda gave her the courage to gather herself and move on. Mom would never have been able to survive without Magda's encouragement. I know that Mom was saved from Ravenbrück and that she was so thin that she only weighed twenty-four kilograms when she took the boat over to Sweden. It was primarily Folke Bernadotte who took Scandinavians sitting in concentration camps, and in the end, they took Jews in buses and transported them from Hamburg in a boat over to Malmö.

This is how Mom came over with her sisters Jölan and Magda. Mom told me she thought it was angels who gave her porridge with thick cream and honey. She ate several plates. Many died like flies. They were buried close to each other the same day. After they showered and were disinfected, they got to quarantine. Mom only got the most vital necessities, and later went up to a camp school in Fjällgården, which was in Hälsingland. They had no idea what had happened to their other siblings. Several years later, Mom learned that her oldest brother, Hersh-Leib, had returned from the war and lived in Grandpa's apartment in Mukacevo. Even her second-oldest brother, Shlojmi, had survived the war and lived in one of Grandpa's apartments in the city with his family. Her third oldest brother, Shoshi, was dead. But they didn't know how he was killed.

Mom told me how she was forced to thin the turnips at Fjällgården and hardly got any food. She also told me that she got some sanitary towels but had to save her pocket money of fifty pennies a week in order to buy anything else. Somehow Mom learned to knit. It must have been Jölan who taught her. Mom sold baby outfits that she knitted to a yarn shop in Delsbo and got together money to buy yarn to knit a warm winter sweater for herself because she didn't have a coat.

Mom also told us that some girls went to the country store to buy eggs, sausages, and other things but that it was difficult for them to be understood. The Swedes could only speak Swedish, so the girls began to cackle like chickens to ask to buy eggs and pointed to their forearm that they wanted to buy something like that. The merchant took out a ham. Another time, they had a man who came with them to shop. They giggled and showed that they wanted to buy sausage by pointing to his fly. Finally, the merchant understood and they wanted to buy sausages. I don't know how long my mother was in Fjällgården, but they learned poor Swedish, little prayers, and mostly how to find relatives that they could move in with and how to find suitable men to marry. Those who had relatives, moved abroad. Those who had the opportunity to study with someone who guaranteed their financial security also did so.

Mom and her sisters had no one to help them, so they had to look for factory work in smaller towns. There was no talk of settling in larger cities. They were not welcome there. So the girls tried working in the rubber factory in Värnamo, which is now Gislaved, where they made sanitary napkins in Mölnlycke. The two oldest sisters quickly married, each their own Swedish. Her sisters called her whenever something chaotic happened. The oldest sister was terribly ugly and had a very poor radiance. She was like one of the king's stepsisters or the goddess Aphrodite after she had lost her beauty and wanted to steal it from Psyche. Mom reminds me of Psyche.

Jölan and had a rough face with slanted unflattering eyes that shifted between gray and green. She had a blunt potato nose and rough skin. She was small with a boy figure. Nothing she said ever made sense. She married a much older man who came from a small town called Lerbäck. They had a son, Bill, who died before the age of fifty.

My other aunt just died, and her fate was the same, but she wasn't as mean as Jölan. Magda married a factory worker and had a son. She became a widow early, and her only son died young. I have had much better relations with Magda. I can see myself in her as a single mother trying to fight with her son Tommy. My cousin always ended up in stormy situations, and Magda always had to help him out of the chaos. He died at forty from cancer.

Magda was never able to deal with his death. She couldn't move from Värnamo because she had to visit Tommy's headstone daily. I can greatly relate to that. Her dementia became severe, and she had difficulty recognizing anyone. She was nursed in a home not far from her house in Värnamo. Magda was buried in the Jewish burial ground in the Forest Cemetery near my parents on December 1, 2013. May she rest in peace.

Jölan was like the goddess Aphrodite, jealous of the human Psyche who fell for Eros. Psyche tries to find her love, Eros, who fled. She asks her sisters to help her, but they refuse. The only one who can help her is the Goddess Aphrodite, who is jealous and wants Eros for herself. She puts Psyche through difficult trials. Psyche passes all three trials and retrieves an elixir of beauty from the underworld. [6][7].

Both aunts were jealous because Mom had the opportunity to move to Stockholm and marry a Jewish man. Jölan made escape difficult for my mother when she slipped away from her alcoholic husband with my father. They had poisoned my mother's existence, so they had to pay by staying in their small towns.

Jölan thought instead that she could get my father. She was the oldest, and when she realized that my dad only had eyes for my mother, the most beautiful sister who was also the youngest, the devil was in her. She went to my mother's former husband and told us that his wife had escaped.

---

[6] Inna's journey by Sylvia Brinton Perera
[7] Anita Goldman, The Love Course (page 92-94)

My mother was treated as a housewife by her Swedish husband, who she had married as a formality to get a residence permit.

When Dad came to Sweden in the middle of the 1950s, he was looking for survivors from his hometown. Quite soon, he learned that there were three girls with the surname Stern who had survived concentration camps. Dad knew my mother's eldest brother, Hers-Leib. Dad looked up my mother when he lived in Gothenburg where he met her through common acquaintances. They fell in love with each other then Mom and Dad ran away together. She was still married to her first husband, but he had several mistresses and treated my mother badly. They fled together.

There is more I do not want to tell out of respect for my mother, who did not want it to come out that she was previously married. Women were treated less favorably by other families at that time, which was very conservative and full of double standards. Now I have broken this promise but told the truth in context.

Mom and Dad took the train to Stockholm and went to the Jewish congregation. They knew no one in Stockholm and had left some good friends in Gothenburg. They did not feel welcomed in Stockholm by the congregation and searched for like-minded Jews who had survived concentration camps. They found their fellow sisters and brothers in the south. They got a temporary residence in Klippgatan and got to know the others who lived in the house. They went to Vitabergsparken and Kungsträdgården where they shared their sorrows and worries. Finally, a need for family overpowered my parents, and they were married at home by the Byk family.

Mom worked a short time for the EPA in the perfumery department and later as a cashier. The Jewish women came and begged for cheaper goods, but Mom had to follow the rules. It was hard for her, and she wanted to help her sisters. There was no chance to start studying. She needed to make money. Dad looked up Broddman and started working at the company. He had hoped to work as a photographer when he had a studio in Gothenburg, but there was nothing he could do. Dad had been used. A short time later, while my mother was waiting for me to be born, they looked for a bigger apartment. The curator of the Jewish congregation did everything to throw them out before I was born. A friend helped Dad get hold of a suburban apartment where their family could grow.

They went to a synagogue located in the south near the Van der Nootska Palace, where they knew their congregation. People tried to support each other there. Many began to work with tobacco stores and sold goods that my dad was not interested in. But the families were desperate, and it was difficult for an eastern state governor in Stockholm in the fifties to get a decent job.

The orthodox character of the area made them feel at home. On Saturdays and major holidays, they went to synagogue. The men prayed downstairs on the ground floor and the women in the stands. Dad brought home bachelors on the Shabbat nights, and Mom had trouble getting the meals together for everyone. Those who came were starving and had not eaten for several days. Mom and Dad felt great empathy for those poor people who didn't have their own families, and the need was great. Dad donated a lot of money to support the synagogue.

Mom and I baked and struggled to make the Shabbat dinner pleasant. Chicken soup was a must. Mom didn't like boiled chicken so it was spiced roasted chicken instead, and it was served with noodles. There were various thin noodles handmade from wheat flour, eggs, and water. We also had gefilte fish, a ground fish dish that included pike, haddock and other fish varieties that were available for the season. It was ground and rolled into small loaves with onions and spices. The salmon was also filled with the ground fish varieties and slowly sweetened with carrots.

We offered different toppings and slow-cooked meat. We often offered goulash, a Hungarian dish with paprika. We drank Pommac and sometimes other soft drinks. For dessert, we often had plum compote made of prunes and lemon cooked slowly with some sugar, or gooseberry compote during the summer. Of course, we also baked fresh challa. Over time, we were given a freezer, which helped with storing the food. I was always responsible for making everything look beautiful. I put a white damask cloth on the table and folded napkins in different shapes, often a fan. I set flowers on the tables and beautifully laid out the cutlery with the glasses. I had a good time with myself. Inanna wounds, grows, and cooks.

Mom did not grow but kneaded, tore, shredded, chopped, fried, ground, boiled, and cooked a lot of food. She always got a lot of praise because it tasted good. Mom cooked as the season's changed, which is the first aspect of the Inanna myth. She put up food and used the fermentation process to refine grain. Mom also made homemade wine out of raisins. It was too sweet for me.

I have described the descent above, and that is the second aspect of the myth. The third aspect is to get out of the abyss and sacrifice some of one's existence as an adaptation to the outer world, to be reborn into a deeper consciousness. She got stuck. The last aspect is to regain power and equality between woman and man.

Unfortunately, there are scars even today in Hungary, and it worries me. After the war and concentration camps, the Russians invaded Ukraine's Crimea with two thousand troops. It is a part of the world that has undergone many stages in sixty years.

My Earliest Childhood
Memories

My first memory is of sitting next to my crib on the floor.

I was playing with my toy dog. It was a small battery-powered white fox terrier. The eyes shone yellowish-green, and it moved towards me. Grandmother had sent it to me from America, and it was one of my first toys. As the first-born, I got the most attention. I knew nothing else then. I also had a rubber doll that looked like a baby. I pointed out that the doll stared too much. I didn't like that.

I remember wearing small white leather shoes that were so soft they almost felt like socks on my little feet. Often I sat and stretched and bent over. Sometimes I took off my shoes and got my foot up as easily as possible. I was like a little bendable rubber doll.

I have a weak memory of locking my mother in the bathroom. I could just reach the key and turned it. I think I twisted the key back and forth until it sounded the best, locking Mom in. It must have been exciting for me that I managed to lock her in, but as a little girl, I didn't understand the breadth of it.

There was a small window in the bathroom, and Mom opened it to shout hysterically to a neighbor to open the door and rescue her. Mom had boiling water on the gas stove and was terrified that I would burn myself. I don't remember if I managed to click the key so she could get out or not. Mom told me that the neighbor she was trying to reach was deaf. Mom was terrified in there, but she came out, and I was unharmed. I think I was over a year.

I don't remember my first birthday party, but Dad photographed me a lot, and I looked like a little princess in a white lace dress surrounded by three boys. I enjoyed all the attention. Mom told me that everyone wanted me to sit on their knees. I don't remember any of this.

I have glimpses from when I started dancing the cancan. My parents had bought a black and white TV, and I looked wide-eyed when something moved. I stood up steadily and began to kick with my legs in a way that reminded me of the dance I saw on TV. Mom and Dad clapped their hands, and I knew I had done something good that they enjoyed. I had cracked the code for getting attention, and when I wanted to be seen, I knew what to do. My parents often visited Millesgården, and among the fine statues, I found platforms where I was high enough to catch an audience.

Tanned with various cute dresses, I danced my interpretation of cancan and got standing ovations from the tourists who were there then. Several American tourists came to my mother and asked to adopt me. Soon my mother absolutely did not want to go there anymore. She took it very seriously. Sometimes I think about how my life might have been different if I'd had the opportunity to be adopted by another family.

My favorite doll was Elisabeth. It was a hard plastic doll with a red velvet dress and brown hair in tassels. I don't remember why, but when I was angry, I pointed at her eyes. Later, I got a bigger doll that I named Elisabeth. She also had reddish-brown hair and a red and green dress, and I liked her better because she was much larger than my first doll. No one has told me why I named the dolls Elisabeth, but I think it had to do with the English queen visiting Stockholm, which even as a child, I had picked up on as an important visit.

I also remember when my little brother came to the world. I was two and a half years old, and Dad got me a box of candies called Pelle Svanslös. The candies were round and had different fruit flavors. The blue ones tasted like blueberries, the red ones like raspberries, and the white I think tasted like mint.

On the big day of honor, Dad took me to Södersjukhuset where my brother was born. Mom held him proudly in her arms, and the first thing I wanted to do was give my brother something valuable to me. I handed him a blue candy. As soon as she saw it, Mother threw the candy away from Danny's mouth. I didn't understand why he wouldn't get to eat the same candy as I did. Dad went home with me, and some days later my mother came home with her baby. I thought I could play with the new baby like my other dolls, but I couldn't. Mom let me be with him when the baby was bathing, and I showed him how to talk. I took the lessons very seriously.

One time, Mom asked me to watch Danny. I don't remember why. Maybe the phone rang or the water boiled over on the stove. I just powdered him a little, but it was too much. The baby turned dusty with white talc and became slippery. He slid down onto the bathroom floor, and Mom came in very upset. She blamed everything on me. How could I have let my little brother fall down onto the floor? How could I be so clumsy?

He could have died. I cried rivers and didn't understand why. I just wanted to powder him like Mom did. It was just too much.

Another thing I remember is large flames coming from the stove at my eye level. I thought it was delicious with all the colors ranging from yellow to slightly blue in the middle of the fire. Mom shouted with hysteria as she saw all the diapers burning up. She had put the diapers under the gas stove. Maybe it was because of lack of space. I don't know, but I remember her fear that we children would hurt ourselves. I think my brother was alive then, but my little sister had not been born yet. Unfortunately, my mother acted from her pain as she couldn't move past it, and she projected her frustration onto me.

I felt disappointed and less important. I was no longer needed. There was a baby that was more important than me. We stayed at the top of Getfotsvägen 88 and had a balcony. I was happy to sit on the balcony and read stories for my friends. Mom told me that my friends did not understand how I had learned to read. I had just copied Mom's way of tracing her finger over the text and pronouncing words associated with the pictures. I watched my friends wide-eyed as they watched me. It looked like I was reading, but I couldn't read until later. I think I was three years old then.

My first purchase was milk. I was maybe four years old and went down all the stairs myself to the street where I walked across the road to the little neighborhood shop.

Mom looked from the balcony and saw me go into the store. She had stood there the whole time waiting for me to come back to the gate. I was really proud of having completed an important task all by myself. Then I carried the glass bottle all the way up the stairs. The first staircase went well, so did the next.

But the last step was another story. I dropped the bottle. It fell from my little hands down onto the stone staircase. The glass shards were thrown out in all directions, and milk splashed over everything. There I stood with empty hands and no milk to give to Mom. I had done my very best, but it had been too difficult. The first Inanna aspect is to receive food. The milk became symbolic to me as it ran down the stone steps.

I began to trade more goods with my mother, which I carried up the two flights of stairs on the Getfotsvägen, and I had to start helping with lighter cooking as a little girl. I have always had to take into account the feelings of others. I was never more important than my poor surviving parents. They had a monopoly on their suffering. Early on, I learned to swallow difficulties biting down the pain and moving on. I got to learn everything about testing my wings.

If I fell, I got up again. Then I tried again without guidance. I had to use my intuition as a child. I grew up with, "Do not disturb dad now." Dad had a hard time breathing with asthma and needed to rest a lot.

It was always Mom who could talk about things on her terms. Often she wanted to talk about the horrors she'd experienced in the concentration camps. "You could never understand what I experienced," she'd say. As a child, I did not understand why I was forced to listen to such horrible stories. I often dreamed that I was in a concentration camp. When I woke up, J would look under the bed and in other dark corners. I became afraid of the dark, and Mom was terrified.

I have an early memory of performing in a Lucia play. I was dressed in a white tunic with a red silk band around my waist. I felt fine with glitter in my hair and a light in my hand. I felt expectant. I knew Mom wouldn't think I was dressed like that. But I went in the Lucia train, and we sang "Saint Lucia" and held our hands together over our hearts. I think we sang to the girls. Maybe other parents were there, but mine weren't.

We had other traditions at home. I had my clothes hook with a blue wing motif. The blue butterfly became a magical symbol for me. It was something beautiful from the fairy tale world. I also remember that we embroidered different stitches. I still have a small white cloth filled with rather complicated stitches that I do not see children of that age do anymore. But back then small children struggled with those types of complicated stitches. I also made a ceramic ashtray of an autumn leaf painted with red against green. But the ashtray broke when I grew up.

At that time, Mother began to tell me more about her war experiences. I started the descent with her, which is the second aspect of the Inanna myth. Mom took us out to the playground where I hit different volts and climbed up onto different climbing frames. I dangled like a monkey. We played and had fun. My younger sister was not as agile. I had to take responsibility for her. I would even carry her carefully. She didn't want to do much herself. If it was too hard, she just would sit down abruptly. My mom was on me all the time about helping my sister. I did the best I could but wanted to touch myself as I liked. I thought it was Mom's role to take care of her.

Once, my little sister took a little excursion into the forest glade to pick flowers. She was with me when I picked paperwhites and bluebells. It was not peaceful. Mom talked to another aunt and trusted me to take care of the Vera. But at that time, Mom had lost track of her for a while. Mom burst into hysteria. We went into the grove, and there sat Vera picking a flower. She literally picked just the flower. She didn't want to take the stem that was near the earth. She thought it was terrible to dig your fingers into the dirt. Maybe she was afraid that an insect would bite her?

Mom did her best, but she ruined so much by telling me about terrors when I was so small. Every child needs security to build a foundation on which to stand. My mother had a tremendous pain because she felt abandoned by her mother.

The deprived mother of everything in a life devastation[1][2]. All potential had been destroyed. Mom had lost control and could not get up. She had lost herself in taking care of me in different ways. She gave me food, clean clothes, and bathed me every day. She showered me with talk afterwards, and it felt good. She kissed and hugged me and tried to tell fairy tales to me. Her accent was hard to understand, but I managed to crack the code. Mom sewed my clothes and knitted cardigans and hats that were really nice.

She loved playing with me but as a child lost herself for a while. She was unable to become more creative and stand on her own feet. She was very moody. Without warning, her mood changed without me being prepared, One moment she was happy and the next she was hysterical or in a rage. Other times, she would ignore me no matter what happened. If I didn't listen to her, she would say ugly words like insulting my eyes and teeth. This became like a mantra, and as a child, I never knew if she would literally beat me or if she was just overreacting. I constantly planned to run away from her if her reactions became too strong.

I remember riding a sleigh with my brother and sister during the winter. It had red seats and was made of pine. Aunt Magda had sent it to us. Mom put us on the sled when there was snow and took us to the sledding hill. We had a lot of fun. My brother went down with Mom. He guided them down safely. She did not dare to go herself. I went down with my little sister.

Then came a neighbor who Mom called to, "*Was sie sagen*." He came from Austria, and I think he always wondered what Mom said. He had a small daughter who had Down syndrome. He saw that Mom was out playing with her three children, and his wife was just sitting at home with her daughter. He wanted to ride the sleigh down. Mom let him go. Uncle sat down on the sled and came down too, but then the sled was destroyed. He did not do it, but just said, "Was sie the case." Then he wasn't so popular with mom.

The time went by, and I started school when I was six and a half years old. I was a really sleepy my first school day. Mom let me sleep late and took me in the children's bike seat. She rode me to school with lightning speed.

---

[1] Inna's journey by Sylvia Brinton Perera
[2] Anita Goldman, The Love Course (page 92-94)

That summer, my brother learned to ride my bike. He was brave. I was out playing as usual and was arguing with my brother. He wanted to take a bike ride and rode away. I could see him at first, but he thought it was boring to just ride a short distance back and forth and wanted to take a little longer ride. Mom was hysterical about that excursion. We found him with the bike a few hundred meters away.

I liked the little trips I took with my mother to school. Then I got my own time with her on my terms. Our teacher Silva came from Germany. I remember her wearing a large dark blue dress with white dots and that she had side-combed silver-colored hair. We were three girls who liked to talk.

A little blond girl who lived in Tallkrogen's villa neighborhood talked the most. Then Helen, or thick Helen as we called her. She was a little girl with brown long hair and nut brown eyes who had a hard time physically running with the rest of us. Helen lived a few blocks from me. I was the third chatty girl, a tall and slim girl with big black curls.

Some days Helen would be heading for school from Gubbängstorget when she saw my mother cycling with me. She would stop my mother and wanted to ride on the bike instead of me. Sometimes, Mom went along with it when we had enough time. Mom would then lead the bike with Helen sitting in the child's seat while I walked with my mother and she held my hand.

Mom came and picked me up quite often and sat at the back of the class with my brother and sister. We learned to read from books like *Mother is Nice* and *The Rose is Red*.

Mom kept her accent. It was the most difficult with the *sh* sounds like in *German shepherd* and *shoot*. One day, we were using a text about rubber to learn to read. When I got home, I told my mother that it was called *rubber* and not *gum*. Of course, she thought she knew better. The next day when we were reading, I said *gommi*. I was reprimanded and told it was *rubber*. So we kept on with different words. In the end, I told my mother she needed to learn better Swedish. I wanted to talk properly.

Mom and Dad mostly spoke Yiddish to us at home, but we children answered in Swedish. I can talk to the older generation who speak understandable Yiddish with a Munkac accent. I did that for many years later when I visited Mea-Shearim, a religious neighborhood in Jerusalem. In the summer of 1980, I met people who spoke understandable Swedish and recognized my grandfather Shreigel as a righteous person. What you would call *tsaddik*.

When we moved, I started second grade at Björksätrakolan. There, the connection between hell and school began. I had a Christian instructor who played the organ at the start of every school day, and every morning, we were forced to clasp our hands and sing hymns.

Do you remember how I mentioned the parallel between Inanna's journey and my mother's story, and how I was her fellow traveler? My own descent started in second grade. As a little girl, I was forced into the dark underworld by alienation. I did not play with the other children because I was a Jewish child. At that time, everyone believed that the Jews had killed Jesus. I belonged to such people, and evil should be displaced with evil. I had to use my premature female wisdom to harden. Somehow I did harden during my days at Björksätraskolan, but I didn't understand why I had to suffer so.

The other children told on me if I didn't sing or clasp my hands. I found a way to bring my knuckles together so that it would look as if I was praying from a distance. I didn't want to clasp my hands when I knew I was a Jewish child with other traditions. The children did as the adults told them. It was the parents' responsibility to teach their children to be kind to all children, but they did nothing to stop this behavior that set deep wounds in my soul.

I had already received wounds from hearing Mom's stories about their traumatic war experiences. My teacher and the children behaved like they were in Erishigal's kingdom where Inanna is suspended on the hook[3][4].

It could be seen as the first victim I needed to do. My punishment was that the children would not play with me on the breaks. We often bathed at home, so it was just plain rudeness to bully me as the kids did. They didn't want to run under my legs when we had such exercises in gym.

The kids in the yard were also special. I was teased for my curly hair. They were incessant with their teasing. The hairs on my arms and legs were more visible because I was dark-haired, and the children teased me, which made me furious. It was much better when I started at Hillelskolan in the city. Then I let go of the suburbs.

Today I passed the place where the gymnasium used to be and saw that it was blown away. Maybe there is symbolism in this? I no longer need to bear these memories of violations by eight-year-olds on these premises. It's gone now. What remains is small cement clumps that testify that there was a building there, nothing more. What happened there between 1965 and 1966 has been removed from the ground in any case.

---

[3] Inannas resa av Sylvia Brinton Perera
[4] Anita Goldman, Kärlekskursen (page 92-94)

What Dad Told Me

Dad had Brit Milah in a vessel made of gold. Grandfather owned a museum filled with beautiful and precious art. Later, he turned the museum into a high school where the students learned Hebrew. The essay "A Study in the Author Sanfrid Neander-Nilsson's View on 'Swedishness'" is despised by the Jewish aristocracy in Mukacevo. They are not comparable with the aristocracy in Sweden.

I am beginning to understand more and more why my parents suffered so much in Sweden when they came as refugees. The aristocracy were examples of the worst kind of Jews. In a video, I heard witnesses say how Dr. Mengele was extra hard on those who came from Mukacevo. He reserved his worst tortures for children on Jewish holidays.

A video I found on YouTube, "The Soviet Invasion of Hungary and Siege of Budapest 1944" by Erdely Magyar, describes what it was like in Budapest. The Soviet invasion of Hungary, called the Siege, was the bloodiest battle in Hungarian history. The district of Buda was invaded after 102 days spanning between 1944 and 1945. By comparison, Berlin and Vienna fell after two weeks and six days of resistance respectively. Budapest was important to Adolf Hitler. It was the capital of the last European country allied to Germany and was close to Vienna. Hitler believed that having Hungary along with an aggressive defense in Poland would keep the Russians off-balance.

Dad lived in houses that Grandfather owned, and Grandmother worked in shops. Grandfather traveled around the continent, and they had good years in Mukacevo until Nazism when Grandfather was tortured to death in Budapest. At the age of eighteen, Dad was trained for *hashara* at a camp that prepared young people to move to Israel. I have photos of him riding on a horse. He told me it was tough.

When the Nazis took over, his possessions were seized, and there were unequal rules for different people in society. It was too hard for Dad. My grandfather was tortured in Budapest by the Hungarian Nazis. They demanded all his wealth before they would release him. Grandmother gave the Nazis everything they asked for as a condition for his release. It didn't help. When they got everything, he was still tortured to death. Grandfather's body was likely thrown into the Donau with many other Hungarian Jews. I found the video mentioned below on YouTube that you can watch that shows all the shoes that lined the quay. One of the pairs might have been Grandpa's shoes that he had to take off before being shot dead and thrown into the Donau. Seeing all those shoes brought me to tears. Poor grandfather. He was on a business trip and trying his best.

Published March 25, 2012

A memorial in Budapest remembering the Jews murdered along the banks of the Donau during World War II. The victims were killed by the fascist Arrow Cross Party. Before being shot, they were forced to remove their shoes. "Shoes memorial in Budapest, Hungary," produced by James Ayala, is a video showing all the shoes that the Jews were forced to take off before they were encased in the Donau.

Dad had to take up the main responsibility for his three brothers and his mother when Grandfather died. I know his two brothers died, but he only told us that the youngest had tuberculosis. It must have been difficult for my father to take over such responsibility. I have no idea how Dad felt when his little brother was ill and did not manage to recover. I do not know how that boy or the middle brother died. Dad didn't tell me. Maybe it was too painful. They were probably shot, tortured, or killed. Grandmother was rescued by Raul Wallenberg in Budapest, who handed her over to the Swiss Embassy. Dad also had a Swiss passport. She stayed in Budapest and was hidden there until the end of the war. Dad went back to Mukacevo. I don't know why he traveled there. He didn't tell me clearly.

It was Dad's hometown then a Nazi took him to prison. Dad made his trip to the underworld as a twenty-year-old. He spent three years in various prisons and concentration camps. I think Dad felt like I was describing in Inanna. "Inanna is killed and turned into meat by Ereshkigal."[1][2] "Everything seems dead", "eyes that nail to life, that get stuck on one occasion or a picture that makes life concrete and static."[1]

Dad had to carry heavy bags and break apart stone. He told us how he was forced to lie in narrow bunks in barracks where it rained and about how the men were forced up from time to time to be counted five by five in appeal. It was like how my mother was counted, but what was different was that Dad got punished. He went up and down carrying the stones in the quarry to no avail. When he delivered his fifty-pound bag, a Nazi would dump out the stones just to be put them back in the bag, so Dad had to carry them up again.

Bergen-Belsen was located in northwestern Germany. The camp started in 1943 and ended in 1945. At best, the prisoners there got a piece of bread and a thin mash of potato skins in something reminiscent of soup. It was full of bacteria, and people fell ill with typhoid. They had to run to the latrines several times a day. Those who were not strong enough to work were killed. I think Dad spent two years doing hard labor and one year in a concentration camp.

Below is information from a video about Bergen-Belsen uploaded on Oct 5, 2010. In the video clip, you can get a glimpse of what it was like at Bergen-Belsen.

---

[1] Inna's journey by Sylvia Brinton Perera
[2] Anita Goldman, The Love Course (page 92-94)

Footage of Concentration Camp at Bergen-Belsen

Initially, Bergen-Belsen was a prison. Himmler converted it to a concentration camp. On April 15, 1945, the camp was liberated by the English. Dad was among those liberated from Bergen-Belsen. He was severely emaciated and had tuberculous and typhoid.

Female Nazis were handed over to British soldiers. They came from the eleventh battalion. Soldiers dragged dead bodies into the moat. The beginning of the video shows how the German Nazis hated the British. But they had no more power to destroy and kill. They had to watch. The dead already looked like skeletons with skins, and the English stood silenced by this horrific sight. They honored the dead and were noticeably moved. Many had difficulty holding back tears. A priest read a prayer for the dead, and the video ended with an excavator filling the mass grave with earth. Watch the video "Bergen-Belsen Liberation."

After, the liberation, Dad ended up at the displaced person's DP camp, which was a German sanatorium where the survivors were treated for TB. My father tried to come to the United States several times but was denied because his lungs were not completely healed. Grandmother greeted Dad, who was the only surviving child of three brothers in his family, then she decided to seek happiness in the United States and get married again.

Shortly thereafter, she emigrated to New Jersey in America. She hoped that it would make it easier for Dad to later come to America. Unfortunately, he was not strong enough to emigrate. He got the chance to come to Sweden and thought that later it would be possible to reunite with Grandmother. I think Dad felt like in the Inanna myth, "Suffering is the only way out."[3][4] The activity is sacrificed, which leads to rebirth and insight when it can be accepted. It meant Dad had to be present in his primitive, dark form—a sense of total loss, even the inability to act, a loss so deep that nothing any longer plays a role, "a place out of the reach of grief." [3] Dad stayed in Germany and spent time with his good friend Bomi, who was in the fur industry. Dad signed up for the University of Prague and wanted to become a doctor but did not get the opportunity.

Dad learned photography and won a photo exhibition with a card from Garmen Parten Kirchen. Then he took the chance and went to Sweden to work in Gothenburg as a photographer and opened his own photo studio. He worked mostly with portraits. He thought going to Sweden would give him a chance to reunite with Grandmother. Unfortunately, my father was disappointed that the trip to Sweden did not lead him to America. "Suffering can lead to a terrible passivity, a negative immobility like the Greek Pirithous who remained in Hades." [3] He was looking for survivors and found my mother who was then married to a Swedish man. They fled to Stockholm. Once in Stockholm, they rented a small apartment on Klippgatan 13. Mom and Dad felt "The pain is because I was abandoned by my mother as a thorn in the heart. And my whole life is dead."[3][4]

Nine months later, I was born at Södersjukhuset on a December morning in 1957. Dad first worked as an assistant for Broddman's photo. The job was at the corner of the concert hall in central Stockholm. The owner drove with Dad. He had to run into dark spaces and carry heavy boxes. He

---

[3] Inna's journey by Sylvia Brinton Perera
[4] Anita Goldman, The Love Course (page 92-94)

developed photographs with smelly developing chemicals that contributed to his breathing problems.

Mom took over the mother's role from Grandmother because Dad was also abandoned by his mother.

Grandmother sent letters filled with her tears. She remodeled the photographs of me and handed in one that was used in an American advertisement. But Grandma never saw me. Grandma did not allow this, and fate wanted something else. Dad cried rivers over not being able to be returned with Grandmother and developed both asthma and heart problems. I remember when my dad rode in an ambulance to the hospital when I was a kid and that my mother was worried.

Grandmother died when I was two years old and, my mother took care of my father, helping him through the grief and loss of his mother. Here I think Mom knew, "Erishigal's hook fills the feminine's generous emptiness with feminine yang strength. It fills the empty uterus and gives the woman an experience of wholeness; a whole which means that she is not dependent solely on husband or child but can be herself full and full individual."[3][4] She couldn't resist the collective and became loyal and pleasant. Mom was not whole but half.

She was dependent on her husband and her children to fill her own emptiness. She became the good mother my father never had. Grandma was as evil and stinky as the underground Aphrodite. Mom took over as the caring heavenly Aphrodite. She clung to the relation, even though it became false and enraged her own integrity. The unconscious cold and the quarrel broke through her control as a result of the sacrifice.

They gave up the possibility of a true relationship to be united with someone, but such an association is simply a way of avoiding confrontations at the expense of their own identity. When it is loaded up enough, the woman falls into depression and this is repeated in a vicious cycle. Grandma was not a good mother. She abandoned her only surviving child so she could have a decent life in America. My step grandfather had two of his own children. I was her first grandchild. Grandmother never saw me and died before my brother was born.

My mother was devastated when my grandmother died. Dad couldn't see her after the war. He had also been stuck to the hook that Inanna made in the myth like the rotting piece of meat and tried to get out of the underworld as initiated. He became passionate about photography and tried to start his life with his new family in a new city. When his mother died, he broke. Mom received his unbridled outbreaks.

Dad tried to get a bigger apartment when I was born, but the Jewish congregation had no mercy. They wanted to get my parents out of the apartment and were willing to split them up. They thought that my father could arrange his own room so Mom could live alone with me. The curator had a stone heart. Somehow, they still got the opportunity to move to Gubbängen, and at the Getfotsvägen, my other siblings were born.

Dad became very sad and had severe asthma attacks. Mom was the sunshine who cooked, sewed, knitted, and played with us children when she lost herself in the present. There is also a parallel between Mother and Inanna as far as their survival strategies. Inanna took flight, and Mom couldn't bear to stay in this. Otherwise, she painted her stories about the war for me.

Dad worked when he was healthy and rested when he was ill. Our first years were spent in Gubbängen on the meadow, playing with other children. I remember when my mother took us to Dad's workplace at the parliament. We walked on the red carpets in the long corridors and men with gray costumes greeted us. I stretched myself to look taller and felt meaningful. I remember the blocks with the pens we got. It made a big impression on me. I think it encouraged me to become good at arguing, which I later used in life.

Dad loved to read, and we had several bookshelves filled with books. He encouraged me to read early, and I often sat with a book on my knee. It was a way for me to relax, a kind of meditation, but also an escape from reality and the horrible stories Mom told about the war.

Dad also told me that I learned many bird names. I remember that I sometimes went underground. I can picture a memory from the blue glass house at Skärmarbrink. It was Folksam's. I don't remember my questions to Dad, but he told me that I asked about the moon and the stars and that everyone listened to his answers. I also remember that we rode the blue tram to Djurgården and that it plunged from the clock. We went up to Norrmalmstorg and then we went on to Strandvägen and over the Djurgårdsbron before stepping off at Skansen. I could walk around in Skansen. After a while, many people followed and listened. I was three or four years old at the time, he told me. I must have felt strange with so many following me.

I remember going to Bredäng and looking at the new house we were moving to. It was muddy, and I wore rubber boots. The house was purple and empty. I thought it looked strange, but Dad explained that it was the body of the house. They would get other colors then windows and doors.

My father was also very interested in politics, and at home, we had lively conversations about foreign and domestic policy. He also worked as an official in the Swedish Parliament. We started to argue about politics when I was young.

He always liked being right. Dad and I also had philosophical conversations about other ways of viewing the world. He had read a lot about philosophy and other religions and worldviews. Later, I understood that his interest was in the Kabbalah.

A good friend of his doctor, Dov Dinur at the Historical Department of Jerusalem, received many books about Swedish Nazism during the Second World War, which he later researched. Before that, it was taboo to mention this dark past.

Good Memories of My School Years at Hillelskolan

The subway began to go all the way to Östermalmstorg, so I started the third grade in Hillelskolan. I did well there. I had classmates that I liked, and I found my first best friend. Anna had long hair, dark blue eyes, and long dark-brown eyelashes. Her father was an Englishman, and her mother had a Hungarian background. I grew up and went to a Jewish school. It was the only school where I really felt at home. There I was seen by teachers and students. Despite the bomb threats, I felt safe.

Yes, there were bomb threats made to Hillelskolan in the 1960s in quiet Stockholm. I didn't think much about how we were more threatened than other children who went to regular schools. I felt I could trust those who watched over us. It became normal that we always had to pass guards before we could be admitted to the school. It was something I did not question as a child. That was how it was, and for me, it became natural to have guards who were there to protect us on the way to and from school.

The year before, I had gone to Björksätraskolan from where I was liberated from Christianity teachings, and when I started in the third grade, it felt like I was in heaven. I was not a stinking Jewish boy. I suffered because the children did not want to do exercises with me in the gym, and they did not pull my hair because I had disgusting Jewish curly hair. At home, I needed to help a lot with cleaning, laundry, and cooking. My little sister and I were Mom's helpers. The days we didn't have school, we needed to help with everything around the house.

Mom cooked Austrian and Hungarian cuisine. There was no fast food there. She baked apple strudel and made a paper-thin puff pastry that had to chill in the fridge for twenty-four hours. Then she grated apples and filled the dough with lots of grated apples, raisins, and cinnamon. It had to be perfectly rolled, brushed, and baked in the oven. There weren't any fast-puffed sugar cookies in our house. Mom didn't think the store-bought dough counted as pastries. Mom always had food ready when we got home from school, and we often brought classmates home with us.

Anna was often at home with me on weekends, and we had a lot of secrets at that age. We drew a lot, and I admired Anna for her nice drawing skills. I remember a special postcard that she sent to me from Amsterdam. Her father, Jan, was employed at SAS, and they traveled abroad a lot on various trips. I was very interested in coming along, but my dad was afraid to let me go with them. He had bad experiences with what could happen to children who accompanied families, and he was afraid that I would be hurt.

Almost every summer, Anna went to New Jersey and a small island that lies between England and France, which seemed to be paradise on earth. There were lush plants and exciting views. I later got to see it briefly when she came home. I received a special purple amethyst ring from her as a sign of our friendship. Anna said it was a magical stone that only existed in New Jersey. The ring was dark purple with blue sparks and was fantastic to wear. When I was a little sad, the ring helped me to get in a better mood. It was unusual at the time for people to go to such places. In the 1970s and 1980s, those who had money for foreign holidays went to Mallorca or the Canary Islands. We did not go abroad on vacation. Dad sent money to various relatives who needed it more. I thought it was unfair.

Every Shabbat, Mom baked challah, and it smelled lovely when we got home. But most of the time, it was paired with a Hungarian meat dish that was slowly cooked about three hours on low heat with paprika powder and onions. With this, she made different kinds of noodles that were boring. She kneaded together the ingredients then tore them into small noodles. She dried them then burned them on low heat with oil. When they were done, they were boiled slowly with a small amount of water. This is the first Inanna aspect. Mom made decisions in the kitchen.

We got many orders from her to cook the food quickly. If we didn't do things fast enough, the dough could be destroyed or a dish ruined. She created stress with our homemade meals in the kitchen. My brother was not allowed to stay in the kitchen. Boys were supposed to do other things, but Vera and I never understood what Danny was going to do. He would polish windows and clean but managed to waste most of the time. Dad had an expression that I never understood where it came from. "Men in the kitchen get fish heads if they help." It certainly came from his childhood.

One of Mom's finest clothes was a purple silk dress. She had bright pink or bright red lipstick and always smelled like Chanel No. 5. We girls also got a drop of the lovely Chanel perfume. I sniffed the scent and found myself in another world. I saw beautiful ladies wearing luxurious dresses surrounded by beautiful exotic places. I closed my eyes for a few minutes and searched for this place in me. I thought I could enjoy living like that as I was growing up. I often dreamed that I married a beautiful and kind man who was tall and strong with brown hair and beautiful blue eyes. He was a businessman who lived in New York, and I had a wonderful life with him visiting beautiful places around the world.

Mom also had beautiful brocade dresses. Dad bought her beautiful dresses when he could, and Mom beamed like a queen. I remember a brocade dress with light green embroidery in different oval shapes, and for this, Mom had matching shoes with a dachshund. Mom had a short-cut hair with height that required extra treatments to get the hairstyle. She tupped her hair to get a small hill that was modern at the time and used hairspray that smelled awful.

I hated her spraying her hair and wondered what the poison in the spray bottles was for. I also remember how Mom put her hair in curlers that she slept in during the night. It must have been a lot of trouble sleeping with those hard plastic rollers. They were pink sticking plastic rolls no larger than one square centimeter in circumference, but they were about five centimeters long, so she had large plastic needles that she thrust through the bobbins.

Her whole head was covered with these curlers with a twisted pink nylon scarf over it, which was in fashion then. Others wore a white French height under a ponytail, but Mom did not go for that. When Mum cleaned, she wore a nylon cap that looked like a bathing cap with decorative ruffles. It was light blue with various roses and white lace that fluttered up with her faster movements when she dusted with the dustbin.

She wandered around like a fast westerly wind. Mom didn't understand why the neighbors were so slow with the cleaning. She often talked to the nearest neighbor who only did a little at a time and drank coffee several times a day. Mom thought that sponge cake was not a pastry. It was something that you quickly twisted with eggs and sugar. She just wrinkled her forehead and shook her head. She did not understand the Swedish way of doing a little at a time and drinking several cups of coffee during the day. If at least it was with pastries, then that would be something to talk about, she thought. Mom often said, "That Maja, she just does a little at a time and rests a lot with coffee and sponge cake. No wonder Swedes live so long." They do not exert themselves, Mom thought.

In the synagogue, she could not shine with the ladies who had sparkling diamonds. Dad gave away much of this money to the synagogue, Israel, and needy relatives in Hungary, Russia, and Israel. Mom was annoyed that she could not shine anymore and that we didn't get any more from the family. I think Dad wanted to get as many blessings as possible. It could be a remnant of his past experiences.

We went to Adat, Israel, a small beautiful Orthodox synagogue on St. Paul's Street. I often sat with my dad and admired the little tabernacle where the big rolls were kept. It was so beautiful with a turquoise roof in a dome supported by Greek white pillars and a purple velvet incline with embroidered lions and Hebrew letters. On the roof next to the turquoise blue dome, the Hebrew reads that we should follow Moses' footsteps. I dreamed of the stories that Dad had told me. I dreamed of Alladin and Sherazade with their beautiful dwellings and exotic decorations.

There were various uncles and aunts with different fates from the war in the synagogue. They did everything to find ways to make money. I especially remember a caretaker who gave us candy bags. We children didn't have to run on the stairs anyway. We were taught early to sit still at the bench and learn to act like adults. It was important to know when we should stand and bow ourselves in different ways. Then it took a long time for all the guys who paid to read out different sections from the tower. It is called to *shnodda*.

Dad hugged a lot, more than Mom thought was appropriate. The ladies sat up in the stands. There was no talk of women sitting in a mixed seating with the men at that time. It was just so in the big synagogue. The ladies also did not get to go into the synagogue down there. There was a kiddush in the front of the synagogue. Where would everyone have room? It was not like today where the rabbi reads kiddush at a clothed table and it is mixed seating. Often someone offered a lighter meal to remember someone deceased, usually a parent. Dad tried to get up from the underworld to the third aspect of the Inanna myth by adjusting to the expense of his existence and trying to reach the world.

Anna and I played the roles of the Addams Family. We often hung out with each other. Anna came over to my house, and Mom made Hungarian chicken with pepper sauce and baked potato, and we enjoyed it. I often spent the night with Anna in Hökarängen and enjoyed her father's jokes and his English accent. Anna got help early on translating texts when the family's finances did not come together. It was Anna's descent through the first aspect of providing her family with money for food.[1] Already, her grandfather wanted her to learn fluent French. Anna started at the French school, and I missed her. We got together in our spare time, mostly on Sundays.

At school, I got really good at basketball and had my classmate Gunnar who trained me to score. Gunnar was a steady boy with big soft hands, steady blue eyes, and a loud voice but had a heart of gold. I was one of the tallest girls and made the goals. It felt very good to make the goals, and I grew out of doing this. It was my first attempt to come up to the third aspect of the Inanna myth. [1] [2] by sacrificing something of my existence to adapt to the outside world. It was too much for the shorter girls who were going to teach me a lesson. They gossiped to Sten, who struck me so that my nose bled.

Sten was a pretty shy boy with blond hair and brown eyes. He got into a fight but was otherwise quite alone. I remember giving him fruit for snacks. His mother often forgot to. It was Sara and Zara who bothered me. Sara had cute little dresses and a cute white fur hat, rabbit I think. Sara had an olive skin tone and dark brown eyes with plain dark brown hair that was short and neat. The bastard Zara had an ugly faux fur hat. Zara was slightly taller and had brighter skin, a sharp eagle nose, and medium brown hair with dark brown eyes. Sara was always kind to me when she was alone. But Zara called her friend against me.

I don't know why, but she already despised me when I was little. She wanted me to remain as a rotting piece of meat on the hook in the underworld to fertilize the soil as in the Inanna myth. She didn't want to let me flourish. Zara tried to get the others on her side. She could be likened to the dark aspect of Aphrodite, who is jealous and wants to pull Inanna down into the underworld. The girls lost themselves and became submissive companions to the dark power of Zara. Sten became the one who had to sacrifice me for them. They pushed me against a chestnut tree and formed an iron ring around me. Sten was encouraged to hit me as hard as he could. He struck, so my nose bled. There, the initiation continued with the descent of Inanna again.

I was terrified of what they would do but couldn't take me off. I didn't understand why the Jewish kids wanted to beat me. I had been beaten earlier by the non-Jewish children and had hoped to avoid it in the Jewish school. I was frozen by shock and could not get away. I stared at Sten, who was forced to beat me to show that he was with them. I saw that Zara was forcing the others to stick with her. The witch cooked a new plot together.

I was bullied by Zara, who would continue to harass me through our school years.

I do not know why, but I think it was based on the fact that I liked someone better than her. I also made goals for my basketball team while she was too short and clumsy to make so many goals. It was the only time I remembered bullying at school during my four years. I don't know what the recess guards were doing. I have no idea why they did not intervene or if we temporarily did not have anyone out in the recess yard. I also can't remember if I dared to tell Miss Marita Pajajausis what happened.

---

[1] Inna's journey by Sylvia Brinton Perera
[2] Anita Goldman, The Love Course (page 92-94)

34

My teacher was Finnish with brown short hair, brown clear eyes, and high cheekbones. She often wore brown dresses and was one of the best. I remember once that I had to leave the classroom because I had talked too much. I don't remember why I did, but I remember she grabbed me by the ear. Otherwise, I have good memories of her. It was rock-hard discipline, and we had to stand in a narrow line without making a sound before we were admitted to the classroom. The same thing in the class. We stood in front of our benches and greeted "good morning," only sitting when the teacher asked us to do so.

Our main subjects were Judaism and Hebrew. My Judaism teacher was Heinz Säbel, a determined German man with high integrity, discipline, and a good heart. I had been prepared at home by celebrating all the festivals. Dad also read us the week's section and explained different interpretations that we discussed at the Shabbat table every Saturday. I always had the highest grades in Judaism and Hebrew. But it was worse for children who did not have parents who kept the traditions in the same way mine had. I remember Säbel asking a question and then we always held up a hand to answer. When Lars got the question, he couldn't usually answer. He tried to find an answer, but he couldn't. I remember Säbel's reaction. "I wish I had a ball of rubber bands that I could bounce from one head to the other so you could answer."

Mr. Säbel said that to all the children who couldn't answer. It was his mantra. For those of us who could answer, it was pretty fun. But I can understand how it felt to those who would get the ball bounced on their head. This was just symbolic, but still.

Lars was a lively boy with mellow mischievous eyes, a brown hat, and he liked to laugh. He was a boy spider, but he always had a good heart. There was also shyness and grief in him. I think his parents were separated. Then came Rechelbach, a Hebrew teacher who had served in the army, and we could feel that. He hit pointers on the bench with quick raps if we were not alert or answered the questions incorrectly.

He was a pretty tall man with severe brown eyes, black hair, and a black moustache that jumped when he got angry. His daughter Alice had started in our class and was quite tall and thick. She didn't have many friends. I tried to be kind to her, so she would not have to feel like an outsider.

I had other friends too. I frequently stayed over with Bettan who lived in a large villa in Mörby and often took responsibility for her little siblings. Her mother was studying to become a librarian. We often picked apples and made applesauce. I also remember that Bettan's grandmother frequently lived there and that Bettan had a Christmas calendar at home. One of her grandfathers was a priest, and her other grandfather was a rabbi, so she grew up with both cultures. Bettan also had to make a descent by taking too much responsibility for her little siblings.

Sarah lived at Birger Jarlsgatan, and her father was the principal. It was her grandfather who owned the photo studio where my dad worked when I was a kid. Sarah always had lots of ink pens that she drew with when the teacher read stories. The rest of us had to borrow the pens for a fee. I think she charged five cents. Already, she showed her business mind. I think she is a psychologist today.

Anna and I used to talk to the conductors in the ticket office in English or French when we were going through the barriers. I was always addressed in English by people who thought I was a tourist.

Rarely did anyone spontaneously say anything in Swedish to me as a child. We gave up after being exposed to this and thought the adults were stupid. We were able to order various pastries in different languages at Sturekatten. We enjoyed when the waitresses didn't understand what we were saying and ridiculed them. We visited museums, exhibitions, and other cultural events that people drove us to as children. Yes, we enjoyed this.

I was tall and fit with blue-black hair and brown eyes with my short blonde girlfriend. People called us chess and dull. When platform shoes came into style, there was an even greater contrast in our height. We were conspicuous.

My parents were very interested in art, and our favorite museum was the East Asian Museum with the Ethnographic Museum coming in a close second. There we went to see tigers and looked with big eyes at the art of different dynasties.

During a party at my home, everything sat around in a ring and had their flower names. The one who was in the middle would quickly find the flower that was named. Erik was often in the middle and had a hard with the cactus.

We who dared to sing were in the Hillel choir. We wore white blouses and blue skirts and sang different songs, which were applauded at various parties. I remember when we performed at the Grand and Strand hotels. It was great. Some played piano or rather tried to play. I sang and got the highest score.

My Teen Years

Then we had the really cool places that were hip near the Whitlockska school in Eriksbersgatan. Leif lived there and adored Tom Jones. Leif was a little gentleman down to his fingertips. He had picked up a lot from his big brother about how to be a man. Leif asked for a chance with me, and we were together for half a day, I think.

When we later went to Palmgrenska co-educational school, it became fashionable to wear midi coats. I begged for a dark blue almost black midi coat that I got along with a black Cossack hat. It was hard to see that I was wearing the Cossack cap because I had big curly raven hair. I was hip. In addition, I obviously had the obligatory blue v-jeans with a knitted shock-pink polo jumper that scratched infernally.

But it was not long before Leif also had a similar midi coat and a Cossack cap. We were a match for each other in our outerwear. Leif tried to imitate his favorite singer with the lingering body language, but it didn't impress me. I thought Tom Jones was a really slimy singer, so it didn't last longer than a couple of hours. I just got angry when I accidentally put on his coat instead of mine.

At the parties, I smelled of Madame Rochas, the perfume Aunt Magda had given to me. I also painted myself fashionably in light pink lipstick and bright blue eye shadow. I snuck on mascara when Mom wasn't looking. Of course, I had matching nail polish in pink with cream pearls. I had various figure-skirts or dresses. Magda sent some clothes, including a jumper and skirt I didn't like. I looked like a twist bag in it. I think it had bright colors like orange, purple, white, and black. Dad said I should choose a bright orange coat.

I didn't wear that coat often. However, when the platform shoes came into style, Anna and I tripped with them everywhere. I had two pairs, one pair had white lacquer with brown platelets. Another pair had all the colors of the rainbow with blue heels.

To party, I wore a pair of brown sandals in crocodile leather with silver heels. It was faux crocodile, I would like to mention. The handbag I remember was a dark blue leather bag that was pressed like lizard skin with a gold-colored chain. Around my hips, I wore chains of different colors, one in shock-pin and one in gold.

One day Ollie came to school and taught us girls how to do makeup. It was Sara's mom. She wanted to do make up for me, but I didn't dare take a seat. Another girl was instead made up. The girls there looked like little ladies.

We had another gentleman. Harry was a great-looking boy with dark-blond hair and brown eyes. He had his eyes on my little sister. One evening, he called our home and imitated Avraham Rechelbach—a thick boy with striped dark hair, blue eyes, and shabby clothes—and asked for a chance with my sister. My sister answered no. He threatened to tell his father, who was a Hebrew teacher and very strict. Vera cried and hobbled for a long time. I grabbed the handset and recognized Henry's voice. I scolded him, and when he roared into the handset, I slammed the phone down.

The Palmgrenska co-education school also no longer exists, but it was located at Kommendörsgatan 13. Some of my classmates from Hillel School continued their studies there, and we ate lunch in Hillelskolan. Leif, Sara, and I continued to Palmgrenska. Sara went into a parallel class. I had Miss Uhr as a class director. She was strict and had a side part in her brown striped hair. She had round glasses and an everyday appearance. She favored Mr. Müller. His father had served in Hitler's German army. It was a feather in the hat of Mr. Müller, who was the yellow pig. No matter how he behaved, Miss Uhr just smiled mildly at him.

Mr. Müller was taller than the other boys and had a pimpled face with steel-gray piercing eyes and short-cut dark-blond hair. He took care of the girls by chatting with them and demanding sexual services. The girls were thirteen, and he was fourteen or fifteen years old. He was especially fond of a blonde girl with long hair that I do not remember the name of. I happened to walk into the class when I saw that he had forced her down on her knees to suck him. He had his fly drawn and forced her head to satisfy him. I felt bad but got stiff as a stick and managed to escape. I myself was a victim and dared not do anything. (Here I think the girl felt like in the Inanna myth. Her garden). "She gives him a good harvest and joy in his bed."[1][2]

I think he was assisted by his helper Urban, a blond boy with gingerbread brown eyes, who thought being an assistant was awesome. When Urban was alone, he made no fuss. On the benches, many of the classmates chain-smoked in a circle. Those of us who did not smoke were still stuck in the circle and got into their cigarette smoke. Sometimes we walked away from the smoking circle. They thought they were tough, but I thought they looked ridiculous with their cigarettes.

Mr. Müller hated me with my big black-haired head and big brown eyes. He picked me as his victim. To the girls standing next to me, he forced me to stink. They held their noses and walked away from me. Miss Uhr saw this but did nothing. I had some buddies who didn't stand up to the freezing. I was terrified about what Lennart Müller and his helper Urban Erikson's could do. Mr. Müller had such great power over all. He knew he was Miss Uhr's yellow pig.

Their noses sniff each other as pigs do with their snouts. I think Miss Uhr was excited by Lennart Müller's manners. Yes, she even enjoyed it. She was perverted. She was ugly herself as a rapier and enjoyed the fact that others were violated sitting there with their tiny, flabby eyes behind round thick glasses, brown striped hair, and average legs and pork. But no one dared intervene when Mr. Müller kicked me and hit me. He pulled my hair. No students helped me then. Miss Uhr knew this. I did not dare tell my parents. They probably had their own war experiences to take care of. Still, I'm lucky that Urban stopped the beatings, and I didn't have to be sexually humiliated like the blonde girl.

This was my third descent into Inanna's kingdom. Against my will, I was humiliated by a Nazi. Here I will try to tie the book together, so you see the red thread between my mother's, dad's, and my own story. My parents were born in a democratic country, the Czech Republic, which was torn apart by chaos when the Hungarians occupied the country. The Hungarian Nazis tormented Jews in

---

[1] Inna's journey by Sylvia Brinton Perera
[2] Anita Goldman, The Love Course (page 92-94)

the same way as the German Nazis. They were lined up. I told you about my parents' fate, and twelve years after the war, I was born in a democratic country that was neutral during the war.

My first seven years were peaceful before I started Björksätraskolan. Yes, I did have Mom's outbreaks and inability to handle her feelings. She stayed as a child in an adult woman's body. Too early I had to listen to her war stories that hurt my confidence in people. Either I thought too much about people or too little. When I started Björksätraskolan, I was also exposed to Nazi-style abuse by children and teachers both physically and mentally. It has characterized me for the rest of my life. Unfortunately, this continued in other Swedish schools.

Of course, I had been subjected to some bullying in the Jewish school, also by Zara who was the trigger. But it can happen similarly in other schools as well. Zara's mother and aunt had also been captives, and she had inherited the evil of tormenting others. I try to understand how this is possible by comparing our traumatic experiences with the Inanna myth and the descent to the underworld. It is a tool that Jungian psychotherapists sometimes use. A therapist recommended that I use it to heal myself from the trauma I described.

Mr. Müller's father was with Hitler and exterminated Jews. My teacher loved her yellow pig, and he was able to beat me with his bumblebee Urban. I thought about how my parents had suffered before they were in concentration camps. I was thirteen then. Mom was fourteen when she rode the train to the concentration camp with Grandma and her little brother. Sometimes I thought it might be Mr. Müller's dad who hit my mother in the head and tore her hand from Grandmother. Here perhaps Mr. Müller felt "As a judge she sits in judgment to determine the fate of the people and to step down those who do not obey."[3]

We were freed from Christianity and had extra Judaism in the center. The best teacher was Nader with his symbolic explanations that I just loved. Then we had a man from Israel who I do not remember the name of. He was a dark-haired man with a beard and black-brown eyes. He murmured in his beard that women should wear long-sleeved dresses and not tight pants. His face turned bright red, and he became excited for the smallest reason. It was unpleasant to have the instruction of the inhibited man. Some students also received tuition and went to other schools.

Unfortunately, there were two boys from my old class from Hillelskolan who were out to get me. I didn't understand why, but they tried to grab me once so I couldn't get loose. It was Putte and Nicklas. Nicklas thought they should tie my legs and wanted to violate me by pushing a glass bottle between my legs into my abdomen. I kicked and tore myself away from these horrible boys. I became strong with some inward force.

I fought and bit them. I spit in their faces so that their gazes were deteriorated. I managed to kick them when I heard Gunnar's voice approaching down the corridor. His voice made me strong, and he saved me from Putte and Nicklas. They were the roots of the deer who reacted to a former classmate. Nicklas was a good friend of Zara.

Maybe she had asked him to do this to me? Mom told me that Zara's aunt and mother had been prisoners in concentration camps.

---

[3] Anita Goldman, The Love Course (page 92-94)

Jewish guards were appointed by the Nazis to control the Jewish prisoners in concentration camps. They fought and punished their own Jewish sisters and brothers and received benefits that let them survive easier in the concentration camps. Mom had seen women whitened by horror and pointed out these women in Jewish contexts. Mom warned me away from Zara. She said she inherited the evil from her mother and aunt. I think Mom may have been right. I felt it when I was struggling to be free. "Inanna is the goddess of war. A field battle is Inanna's dance and when she gives victory she is with the choir in readiness at the peak of the battle in the warrior's arm. She possesses the wild instinct's energy that was later attributed to Artemis in Greece. She is described in a poem as "all immersive in power, attacking as an approaching storm, with terrifying sensation and a twisted heart."[4]

Nicklas was a skinny boy from Örebro with blond hair and protruding ears and eyes. He did not fit into the class and reacted to things in strange ways. Later, he became active in the center with administration and continued various assignments in the Jewish congregation. This also continued into his teens on the initiative of Zara. I do not know, but I think Gunnar saved me from Putte and Nicklas that time. Gunnar also helped me with coaching basketball and popping in the goals. Gunnar was then the strongest boy from the class. He did a lot of slaloms and won in arm wrestling. I felt strong when Gunnar chose me of all girls to coach basketball. I admired him and saw him as my mentor, like a big brother I never had. It was hard to shoulder the burden of being a big sister. Gunnar trained me in arm wrestling, so I would be strong. I needed this later.

I'm grateful for the support Gunnar gave me when I was growing up, but it aroused envy in Zara. She had a strongly marked hawk nose. In middle school, I almost won over all the guys in the class. It was only Adam and Gunnar that I didn't win over. Putte was a small brown-haired boy who was quite kind when he was alone. He had sparse teeth and light blue eyes and married his girlfriend early.

There was a special girl who wanted to get attention but didn't, and that was Zara. In addition to her sharp nose and striped brown hair, she had a boy-like figure for a long time. Not until long into her teens did she gets small forms. She tried to imitate her best friend's clothing style, but she was pretty thick, and the clothes looked bad on her little chubby figure.

Her best friend Sara got to play Snow White in the school play but not Zara. I think I had to be Sneezy, but I didn't care. Already, I had good self-esteem. Zara went to Gubbängskolan and flirted eagerly with all the boys. I started in Gubbängskolan when the bullying was too heavy in Palmgrenska Samskolan. Unfortunately, I was put into Zaras class. She was fatter than in middle school. Now she had improved her clothing style and had received an allowance to buy clothes. She had green gabber pants that were flared with marking tops. Now she wanted to show that she had lost weight. She still had a boy figure in size forty with tiny breasts.

Her nose was as sharp as before, but she marked her eyes heavily with mascara. Her eyelashes looked like tiny ink pumps around her watered-down brown eyes. Her thin, lifeless, almost

_____

[4] Inna's journey by Sylvia Brinton Perera

transparent lips clenched when she saw me join her class. Immediately, she tried to freeze me as before. I didn't care much.

She had a best friend Berta, a short little girl who had a good laugh. She had short brown hair and blue eyes. I let them be kept. I still had my friends who lived in the city that I went to parties with. Zara was not often invited. I also had some friends in the class. I spent a lot of time with Anna on the weekends. We danced Israeli folk dances and performed at the center and other Jewish events. We had our admirers there at the dance.

I had Anders, a tall man with olive-colored skin, dark brown eyes, and licked hair in a style like Gregory Peck's. My mom thought he was like him, and he was one of my mom's favorite actors. Anders did everything to look good and be popular with both my mother and me. One problem was that he was ten years older than me. When I was fourteen, Anders was twenty-four years old. as a girl of that age, I thought it was disgusting. Anders was always there and helped when the music stopped working in the gymnasium where we danced, but it did not help that he always helped me with my chair when I sat down at the table. He was always so polite.

Anders was with me since I was a year old, and he was with my mother when she married. He was determined to marry an equally beautiful bride. I reminded him of my mother, and he had already decided. But I hadn't. Anna had a stalker and she called him pea. His name was Arthur. He is a short very plump man who was ten years older and admired Anna.

Like Anders, he tried to set the chair when she sat down. So there we sat, ladies at the age of fourteen, courted wherever we were.

We danced Israeli folk dance for a few years with Zoltan and his brother. We thought it was fun. Anna sewed a red skirt, and I had long trousers and danced in the man's role in the dances. We danced as couples often in a circle and then it was good that we had different roles. I was not so fond of dancing as a guy, but I was taller, and it was more natural that I took that dance role. There was a big height difference between us.

I remember that a counselor had asked my parents how it was at home once. I had an extremely thin period. I had gone down to forty-eight kilos. I'm pretty tall, so I looked very ravaged. Then Mom came up with a suitable answer that I was allergic to various things. It was true that I was allergic. They had gone with me to a doctor, but it was the detergent I was allergic to, and they bought a soap for me to wash my clothes in. It was a square-shaped mild French soap called Le Chat. I soaked all my clothes in the bathtub, and then I washed my clothes with the soap and rinsed the clothes thoroughly before drying them. But I didn't get any better.

I think I suffered from severe stress and got severe skin erosion over my body. I do not remember if I was tested for different food allergies, but I would not eat some nuts. It was so extreme that the school nurse said I had to eat everything. The first thing I did was take a piece of almond paste and eat it greedily. A few years later, I vomited breakfast every day before going to school. I was forced to go into the science track in high school. Dad wanted me to be a doctor, and that was the track that was a prerequisite for moving on. The whole semester, I vomited. I now understand that I suffered from bulimia. When I got to change my direction to the economic track, I felt better, and the vomiting stopped.

I started in Frans Schartaus high school. An older guy there liked me, and he carried me everywhere. It was embarrassing. I didn't want to be carried over everything. The mistress noticed this, but Bo charmed her, so he got her on his side. Today it would be called sexual harassment. There was no such expression as sexual harassment in 1974. I remember being afraid of what Bo could do if I gossiped or said too much. Bo knew Zara, my tormentor.[5] They had met in the Jewish center. There she worked to earn extra money. She had met Bo there, and I guess the witch asked the devil to harass me. Why else would he do this?

In the summer, I started my first job at a post office. I started out earning five kronor an hour and worked at Drottninggatan. I saved the pennies to take my first holiday abroad. I worked the summer at the post for eight kronor an hour. With the hard-earned pennies, I got to go with my mother to Budapest to visit my cousin and see a little of Europe. We traveled for more than one and a half days through Europe. I remember how it irritated my stomach. The first stop was Sassnitz, where we left Scandinavia. At last, I was traveling abroad with my mother for myself. I was looking forward to the holiday.

When we switched to the Yugoslavian train, conditions became dirtier. We were offered Turkish coffee, a strong coffee that just tasted like a swamp. Mom wanted real coffee. The spoon stood for itself in the coffee mug, so I agreed with her. We mostly stayed in our own cabin as it was so dirty everywhere. When we came to East Berlin, inspectors came into the train and asked for our passports. Mom was angry. She was afraid that they would drag her off the train because they could see that she was born in Munkacevo.

I comforted my mother and said, "Mom you are a Swedish citizen. They can't do anything. Calm down."

It was her war experiences boiling up. She didn't calm down until we got to the Czech border. The next stop was Prague. The same thing happened again when they wanted to check our passports. Mom was as scared in 1974 as she had been during the war. Eastern Europe was communist. It was not as popular to go to these countries as it is today, so you should familiarize yourself with how it was at that time.

Mom calmed down again until we got to the Hungarian border where the guards asked again for our passports. Again, mom was scared, and I calmed her. When we arrived in Budapest, a red-haired lady came and met us. It was Dad's cousin Itsa. When she took off her coat, I saw an evil dress. Everything was screaming red. She immediately checked what we had with us. To get something of value at that time, goods were required to sell on the black market. For that, she could switch to dollars and buy something in the coveted dollar store. American jeans were desirable, but there were none in our suitcase.

The brewed coffee was the instant coffee that was popular. She was extremely greedy for being Dad's cousin, and we didn't enjoy staying at their home. What we did was register with their police when we lived temporarily there. The thoughts that came up about the war became too much for Mom. She began to moan. I comforted her, and we went on long walks.

---

[5] Inna's journey by Sylvia Brinton Perera

We found a pastry shop that served Austrian-Hungarian cuisine. We sat and enjoyed the finest pastries we could buy for some forint, the Hungarian currency then. When we got home, we said we had found the pastry shop. We were told that it cost too much, and we should not indulge ourselves. Dad's cousin wished to lean on us about everything. We took her on one of our walks once, so she could show us the other neighborhood. It was Budda, and we looked at a Carmen set. It was very beautiful. But when we needed to go to the toilet, we had to pay for it.

Dad's cousin again said it cost too much. My second cousin took my mom and me to an amusement park, and I went on the roller coaster with him. I did not understand that my dad had plans for him to marry me and come to Sweden. Robbi was a doctor, and it was quite possible to get a job as a doctor here after a supplement. Robbi thought we should get married and have five children. He was a gynecologist and said he could help me have them.

It was too much for me. I ran from there on my long slender legs, sobbing. How could Dad have a plan for me? To marry me to a relative who was ten years older? I didn't know him and didn't want a lot of kids. When Robbi realized that I didn't want to marry him, he bought me a Hungarian doll with tassels as a gift. I never liked the doll. It looked at me coldly with its enamel eyes. The dress was beautiful with purple outlined with Hungarian flag colors and lots of tassels on the bonnet.

We went to the country to a summer cottage near Lake Balaton. It was a healthy bath. The clay lubricated and nourished the body. Mom and I sunbathed on the roof and picked sun-drenched apricots from the treetops that were trimmed to just the right height to be picked by us. We smiled and enjoyed sunbathing in the sunbeds. They took care of the fallen fruit, grinding them into a slimy mass. There would be juice from this then she said.

She was angry with us. Dad sent money to Robbi as a doctor and had supported the family financially for years. Instead of being grateful for the support they had received, she was rude and demanded more. She was boundless.

I got to know the neighbor girl who lived near the cottage and was nice. Itsa said it was her husband's brother's country house. Then her husband came limping in, dragging his leg. I felt sorry for him. He said his brother was Christian Dior. I replied that it was not possible. He is French and the most famous designer in the world. The man told us that his brother did not want his Hungarian descent known and had dictated a story about being born in France. Dior means walnuts in Hungarian. They met in secret. When they arrived in Budapest, they lived in a luxury suite and only the most famous people met them.

I didn't believe him, but when I exchanged letters with the neighbor girl, she told me about the campaign that would come to Sweden through a famous boutique. I began to believe that story. Why would the neighbor girl write about this? Her father was a senior doctor, and they lived a better life. She had nothing to do with my dad's cousin.

I started studying more at the Frans Schartau's trade school after the summer vacation. There were lots of topics I needed to catch up on, so I had a break with the Israeli dance for a year. I mourned it, but I needed to read more about business economics and accounting.

I had large knowledge gaps to bridge. There I met Kia, who I still spend time with. We supported each other's second year. Kia was in love with her boyfriend. There was no talk that I would meet any boy who came home and stayed with my parents. Her parents were more open, which separated us. I do not remember much of the second year. I only did the spring term class.

I didn't like to write on the typewriter. It wasn't a tool that worked for me. At that time, it was about knowing where to put my fingers. The pages ended up full of Tipp-Ex, and there were far too many gaps in what I wrote. I understood that I could not use it in my professional life.

I didn't like the report any longer with all the details and debit and credit. I do well with mixed right and left with the accounts. In my checkbook, I wrote up the accounts neatly in T-accounts. I learned how to balance them together, much like knowing what is plus and minus on a battery compartment. If you don't see the markings, it's hard, but it is at least marked there even though it is hard to see in the black plastic. With T-accounts, one would know in their head which is the negative side and which is positive.

Then there was distribution, which was about selling things. It was also not what I wanted to do, but I didn't know about management, so in the fall, I decided to try the direction of management. Kia took the linguistic orientation, and she focused on secretary jobs. It was mainly the intriguing Zara, who wore Dior bags, that became interested in me. Someone told her that I had lived in Dior's holiday home one summer. She was green with envy.

In the third year, I was in the same class as my agonizing Zara. Why would this woman choose the same direction as me? She manipulated and destroyed me all year round. She started to sleep over with a boy named Bert. It didn't stop her from sitting on the laps of other men and yelling with the other guys in the class. She was voracious and read all the literature about sexual deficiencies. Zara teased me not to be as liberated as her. At home with me, she lived orthodoxly.

My parents went to the little Orthodox synagogue in the south and kept strict on kosher and religious celebrations. Her parents didn't follow many rules. Kosher rules dictate what meat, fish, and other dishes are okay to eat in Judaism. In Sweden, it is particularly difficult. It is expensive and difficult to obtain strict kosher food. It is also forbidden to slaughter animals according to these rules in Sweden, and it creates difficulties for people who want to practice their religion. Zara gambled with the classics yellow piglets Jörgen and Mia. Jörgen was five years older than the others, and his parents were lawyers. He was motivated to get the best score and studied hard with good results. It also made them and Mia become the fat teacher's favorites.

Sune Eklund was a heavily overweight sports teacher. He was also my class director. He was old and very conservative in his approach. The girls who did sports did not receive any assistance from him. However, the guys got lots of extra benefits. In the same way, he gave Jörgen extra points on writing as he told me loudly and clearly how he deducted points on my writing to give the point to Jörgen. The reason was that my writing was greedy. It was non-female and illegible.

A woman's handwriting should be small and neat according to Sune Eklund. I admit that my writing is sloppy, especially when I'm stressed. But deducting points and telling me off in front of other classmates is crossing the line. I was too scared to complain. I think I only dared to go to the headmaster once to complain about the class director. He had created such a swamp. Why didn't I know? Perhaps there was fear of him that made people not want to cross him?

Class director Sune taught legal knowledge. I remembered his stupidly specific hypothetical questions that we had to learn. Why was it important to know which land areas were important? Why was it important to follow the law when it came to wild boar binging on acorns in the forest? You can hear how cowardly it was. The fat teacher might have been anxious about dietary regulations. Instead, he recommended we sit in the coffee shop and drink coffee with a pastry and solve his assignments on legal knowledge.

He harassed me because I didn't look feminine. I would look at Mona, how feminine she was with her shiny hair in a pageboy hairstyle. He emphasized that her painted red nails with matching lipsticks and clothing style were better suited for a woman. How could I just look like I did with my curly hair and masculine clothes? Besides, I was unmade. The old man was too horrible.

I wrote a special piece about "The struggle for women's development in Sweden." It was the International Women's Year during my third year of high school. My dad thought it was a good topic to write about, so I started to study this specialty. There was no Internet at that time. It was very radical then, with red support socks and everything that I examined. It was very inappropriate to write about something so radical in a conservative school. Frans Schartau's trade school dated back to the mid-1800s with an educational program for boys that had a commercial focus.

The women had to fight to enroll there several years later. That's probably what disturbed Sune Eklund most. The summer before I was in France, and I didn't think I needed to care much about my appearance. I wanted to be seen for who I was. It was my teenage revolt. Boys and men had been running after me for my appearance since childhood, and I wanted to be chosen for the person I was. My revolt began before the third year, and I decided to become less vain.

In addition, international women's year was celebrating equal rights. To be clear, I was not on summer holidays in a feminist camp, on the contrary. I was in a Benej Akiva camp in Normandy. The castle we lived in is called Chateau de Grumesnil. There, Jewish teenagers from all over Europe met to share common values. It was nice to get to know other young people.

I also remember how the girls knit frenetic jerseys on the breaks. Perhaps it was a way to keep their nerves in check instead of smoking. I did not have the patience to stick to it then. I got that much later. They were also influenced by the old man devil.

Then I had Tor Wertseus,(Totte) who was my main teacher in management. He was a teacher I looked up to. Totte, as he was called, had an MBA in politics and worked extra as a board member in various courtrooms. He seemed to speak from the heart. He did not look like much to the world. He had one eye almost closed, and his mouth was distorted. He was sociable and distinguished himself from the other super-conservative teachers. He was a cat among pigeons in that fine old school. But he had a heart of gold.

My strongest memory is of a film he showed about the mentally handicap. I think it came from something called R-pocket. The emotional movie grabbed me. It was an interview with parents who had to leave their child who had Mongolism as it was then called. Today, one says Down's syndrome. It was so sad to see these parents who had prematurely aged. They went there bent by shame to meet their disturbed son who lived away from them in an institution. Some cut the connection abruptly. It was recommended by the staff at birth. I didn't understand then that it would be my fate later in life. It was so horrible what I saw in the movie. I didn't think I was going to have to deal with anything so terrible.

Do not misunderstand me. I am grateful that I had the opportunity to finish my high school years at the school. I became a high school economist and could have bought a nice gold ring that almost looked like the business school's graduation ring. Unfortunately, I did not have the grades I deserved due to Sune's reduction of my tests due to my writing. He also said that he would influence how the other teachers graded me. That made the old man a devil. Zara also did everything to destroy my future prospects by avoiding giving me information about homework I had missed when I was ill.

Or she gave me the wrong information so that I read the wrong pages before writing. I was too naive to understand the breadth of her evil when I was a teenager. She stayed up half the nights to pound the knowledge in her head. It was mostly to learn what the photos in the books showed.

It wasn't until I went to the university that I was allowed to really analyze and use my words. In high school, I had still needed to help a lot at home with household chores like going shopping for heavy boxes of food to stock up on. My sister had to do the laundry, carrying heavy cloth bags with dirty clothes then washing, drying, and folding them. We had to vacuum, dust, and scrub the floors and cabinets. It took me a lot of time.

Once when I had an important test to do, my parents thought it was more critical that the house was spotlessly clean because an important guest from abroad was coming to visit my parents at home. The usual cleaning was not enough. Now every carpet fringe had to be in place. My siblings and I sat on each side of the carpet edge and straightened the lashes. Dad stood watching us with critical eyes. I remember then that my brother also helped with the carpet fringes. Otherwise, he was free of most of the chores. Carpet beating was also his lot, but my sister and I also had to beat the carpets. They were heavy oriental rugs that had to be rolled up and carried down to the yard. There they were rolled out on a ground to be dragged around and beat. It was great for us girls to do. If we did not clean properly, we would have to sit in the shambles for a while and wait.

It was not easy to make time for all the heavy tasks at home. In addition, we were children responsive to every little reaction Mom or Dad gave. We knew that the smallest thing could tease gall fever from our parents. I didn't want to be punished. I got hard bangs on my head. My hair came loose if I didn't listen to what my father said. Not paying attention was enough to get my face slammed or back kicked. His special torture was to have me pull down my pants and get hard lashes with the leather belt over my butt and back. If we didn't do as he said, it just got worse. Dad was obsessed with anger when he had these aggressions. Often it was Mom who told him something that disturbed her, and Dad was forced to punish my siblings and me. It was he who had to take that responsibility. Mom played the role of good, but it was often she who gave us to Dad. She was as involved as he was.

I believe that my fibromyalgia broke out because of all the hits I received from my father and the agonists I had in school and later in life. Then my mother asked my dad to stop beating us. He couldn't stop once he started, and she could play the role of the good one. She should have taken responsibility for her shortcomings instead. But she couldn't.

Mom was a victim who could not take responsibility for what she had been through to seek adequate help. She could also not take responsibility for the fact that we children were abused at home and seek help for us either. She was ashamed and silenced by this.

I wrote poorly on the sample and was ashamed. I always needed to tell Dad my results. I was penalized when my grades were not sufficient.

There was a show of hands in the class when the class director asked where parents were working and their job's phone number. When it was my turn, I became embarrassed I didn't have the number for Dad's job. He was just a simple administrator in the parliament, and I was offended. Periodically, Dad was sick and at home, so I state our home number.

The parents of the other children were fully healthy. Most were self-employed and had good finances. It was obvious by how my classmates were dressed. Zara used her entire study grant to buy clothes, and she worked extra on the weekends to keep up with fashion. I didn't.

I had also gained some weight at the beginning of the autumn term. The French cheeses had tasted a little too good in France during the summer vacation. I also wanted to get a fuller bust and thought if I gained weight I would. Mom commented that a woman's pride lies in having rich breasts. She didn't think I had full enough breasts, but I had had a perfect balance between my body parts before I became fuller. Mom was pretty short with a boy figure and huge hanging breast. That was nothing I wanted.

I was in my teenage revolt then and did not care. We went on a study trip to Falun, and I lost weight until I had a normal figure again. I don't remember what we studied, but it was something about management. I tried to get inspiration from Totte and thought if I was studying masters in politics at the university I would get a good job and respect. I checked out a new lead on public administration and applied to the university. I got in and was very happy.

The following year, I did excellent the first year and visited Frans Schartaus again. The old man came stealthily with his sports clothes and saw that I was hugging two other teachers. They were very happy that I managed so well. They had been my teachers for business administration and Swedish. Sune Eklund did not greet me. I yelled at him. Watching points, I managed to get into the management track and completed the first year with high marks. I was going to get an MBA in politics. He was embarrassed, and I enjoyed the revenge. The old man's devil failed to destroy my future.

My Chance of a Redress

When I was sixteen years old, I thought it was time to go to a Valborg ball at the Strand Hotel. I think it was 1974 or 1975. I remember Mom helping me sew a long black skirt. I had a festive blouse with several straw folds in nougat color that could pass for gold. Anna also wore a long skirt. Her uncle escorted her to Östermalmstorg, and from there we girls walked the short distance from Stureplan to Strand Hotel.

We saw all the happy people at Birger Jarlsgatan quickly passing by in different directions. We giggled, high on expectations of how the evening would be. Later I was told that my parents had met with Anna's uncle at a restaurant in Östermalmstorg to discuss what they would let Anna and me do at these types of events. Mom told me that her uncle was expecting my parents to pay for everything, and she thought he behaved greedily.

I remember that when Anna and I stepped into the Strand Hotel, we were greeted by a red velvet rug and a romantic, festive glow. I wore the Miss Dior perfume that smelled of lily of the valley and felt stunning. We walked up the stairs and saw people mingling with each other. Most of them were a few years older than us and came from families that we did not spend time with.

After a while, I felt as if my clothes were not nice enough compared to the other ladies' designer dresses. They look at Anna and me as if we were crazy kids crashing their party. We felt their disapproval and walked around trying to find people we knew. We ended up sitting mostly by ourselves and giggled.

After the meal, it was time for dancing. The ladies sat along the wall looking at English tapestries while waiting to be invited to dance. We didn't sit long before Anna was invited by David's brother, and soon I was invited by David. He was tall and handsome with a charming smile and had a carnation in his jacket. I was very pleased to be invited by him. Most of the men were shorter and rounder.

David was quite stiff and went two steps to the right and left then rode quite robustly forward. But I didn't care. The panel hens were watching us dancing and stared for a long time as we danced and talked. I enjoyed every minute of that attention. Surely they wanted to know what David was so fascinated with. It wasn't enough that I was sweet. I was not made-up according to all the rules of art like them. Certainly there was a makeup artist who came to those divas' homes and made them up before the party. The only makeup I could do was my blue eye shadow, pink lipstick, and pearly pink nail polish.

The nail polish was Cutex. They certainly used Dior or Chanel. However, I was proud of my Miss Dior perfume, which sent the right kind of signal. Then it was important to make an impression on a young man in order to have the opportunity to marry a few years later. That was why the divas were dressed up like they were. Their future was set out. I wanted so much to fit in, but I did not always have my footing with education and work. That would come a few years later when I became considerably more confident with my academic degree, which was my entrance ticket to a better self-image. It didn't help that they had their nicely designed dresses.

David asked me how I thought the party was, and I smiled at everything he said. I didn't tell Anna very much of what had happened as we went home together. We had been through a fantastic experience. Anna was perhaps not as thrilled to have danced with the short chubby brother, but I was happy. David's family had a good reputation and was well financed through their work in the fur industry.

After a few months, he invited Anna to a student ball at the Van der Nootska Palace. We were invited by his brother who happened to come across us at the center. We didn't buy long dresses for the ball. I had a pretty short pink skirt, a cute blue blouse for, and white platform shoes. Anna also wore a short skirt with a blouse, but we were the only girls with short skirts. Everyone else wore the right clothing, but it didn't matter. We were there. We danced and had fun.

After college, David went to Israel and worked as a diamond grinder. He came home to Sweden from time to time, and we sometimes met over the years. I went to other parties and met other men who I ended up dating, but I didn't fall for anyone during my study years. Most of the guys were ugly and uninteresting.

I do remember a guy who impressed me at a party. He saved me from a clumsy man who ran after me after the party. We went for a date to eat, but it bothered him that I stuck so strictly to kosher dietary rules. He teased me and ordered pork. I felt great distaste for his arrogance. We were both Jews, and he could have done better. It wasn't that he was uninterested in me. He just wanted to make me uncertain. Despite his behavior, he called me to say that he would like to get closer. He didn't impress me.

These men didn't care what I liked. They didn't even listen. They were only concerned with my appearance and just wanted me as a trophy. But I scolded their idiotic invites, and they had to look for others instead. I knew many others who would anything to get along with some guys, like many teenage girls today. But as a teenager, I was already an adult in many ways and thought it was childish. I wanted to decide my own feelings and what I wanted to do with my body.

Zara, as I mentioned, already had a boyfriend but was into all the sex games that existed at the time. She eagerly told me about them then sat on the laps of other boys. Many of the girls were slow and thought they would be accepted if they engaged in this behavior. Some became pregnant and got married young. Others did not get married and had to find other solutions. Zara had to go pregnant to the synagogue where everyone was Orthodox and knew that she was not married. It was quite unusual in the early 1980s to behave like this. She married in the eighth month of her pregnancy after much persuasion.

I was very proud of myself. I would go in Totte's footsteps, the gracious teacher in management who became pol mag and dared to go against the goblins with the extreme views. I matured several years inside. I showed that I would do well even though the old man destroyed my last year of high school.

At the university, I was the youngest in the management track at nineteen, and we had a lot of group work and seminars. The lectures were scattered, and we needed to quickly get into the academic world by understanding how our teachers perceived economics, political science, and statistics. These were not subjects that I read about in high school, so I just did my best.

I ended up in an odd group where we would do assignments and seminars. One lady, Inger, was twenty years older than me. She was a mother of three and extremely left radical. She voted for Kommunistiska Förbundet Marxist-Leninisterna (KFLM(r),the Communist Leninist revisionist party, which no longer exists today. In the group were also Ida, a silent student from Norrland who did not dare to say much, and another man whom I forgot his name.

The style then was beak boots with puffy velour clothing mahjong and Palestinian scarves. I wore gabardine pants with tight shirts, which were a completely different style, and my political views were also completely different. I was smart enough to keep quiet when it was completely useless to have an opinion in the group.

Inger dominated the group's appearance. There was another group with a similar style to me, but they already had enough members in their group. Oh, how I wanted to change groups. Still, the first semester went pretty well as the subjects were new to many. There was a click with the sisters who knew exactly what they were getting into. They were children of the then ministers of the government. They also knew that they would continue to work on political tasks within the Social Democratic Party.

I tried to find a student room to get a study. When I finally had to move to one in the vicinity of my parents' apartment, competition got stiff. Most were reserved for those who needed them more, those with social problems.

Okay, I had to wait. It gnawed at me. We had to do a lot of group work and visited each other's homes to get better study opportunities. The university was not inviting.

It was an ice-blue glass house and the rest was green, more like a hospital with a library than an institution. Inside, there were white walls and uncomfortable plastic chairs that were color-coded between the institutions. I often read in the A-house but also in the B and D-houses if I remember right. The university area was not so extensive with different pavilions then. The building echoed, and the noise destroyed our concentration. For hours, we sat on the awkward chairs, which were placed between the floors, and tried to solve the tasks when it was my turn to stand for the local.

We ate in the yellow villa. It was a dilapidated ruck a few hundred meters from the Frescati building. Their dishes were homecooked and full of fat. There was nothing I liked, and no variations to choose from. It was either sausage made with lard or something else disgusting to eat. I was happy when I found something else because I was a vegetarian at the time.

Unfortunately, there were no opportunities for me to invite my fellow students to my parents' apartment. It was inappropriate from several points of view. It was too crowded, and my parents had been upset to see Inger with his Palestinian scarves and hear her extremely left-wing views.

I remember a winter day when Inger thought we should jog around the track to get more energy.

Inger wore her cozy pants and Palestinian scarf; Ida wore tight jeans and rough boots, and I jogged in the difficult terrain. We barely managed the shortest distance. There were lots of slippery pits and lumpy mounds. We came up wearing red sweatpants just before a group report in the political science seminars. Our teacher, who was a distinguished man in the dark gray suit with a black polo jumper, looked at us with surprise as we stepped into the hall. He told us to come in.

Inger replied yes, saying we had just run the track to get some energy. The teacher shook his head a little, so subtly I almost missed it. Then there was the account of some task I had long ago forgotten about. So continued the first year. Group work at Inger's home continued, and she brewed the Norrlandic coffee so strongly that the spoon almost stood up in the mug. She liked that it would wake us up though it was mostly her who nodded off. Inger had no empathy and enjoyed the attention.

One day my cousin called me.

"Hey, it's Bill."

"Are you okay?"

"I'm fine," Bill replied. "I heard that you were also studying on the public administration track."

"Yes, I do."

"Why do you do it Why do you have to mimic me and study the same thing?" Bill asked.

"What do you mean?" I replied. "I have no idea why you are studying management, Bill. I think you are evil calling and accusing me of imitating you." I hung up on him.

Bill's closest study friend's girlfriend was in the same year as I was on the administration track. Bill found out how my studies went through Gunnar. I was terribly angry that Bill phoned me and poured out his accusations. Then the plot was running. Bill checked my results from the exams and reported to Jölan, who was the nasty aunt I described in the chapter What Mom Told Me. She was mean to my mother. Now the aunt got water on his mill and called my mother to complain. She got a mouthful from my mother.

Another time, Aunt Jölan called my mother and I answered.

"It's Jölan. Quickly give the phone to Mom. It costs a lot to make international calls."

"How are you, Jölan?" I asked.

"I want to talk to your mother," Jölan answered.

Mom took the phone and said, "Hello, it's Malvina."

"Have you heard?" asked Jölan. "Pia mimics Bill."

"No, she doesn't," Mom replied.

"It's Bill who mimics Pia."

"Are you not sensible?" Jölan answered.

Mom got hysterical then opened her eyes. I knew what that meant. My aunt was crazy as usual.

"Now you have to stop, Jölan."

"Bill studied at the School of Economics last."

"Why has he stopped?" Mom asked. "I didn't know he stopped."

"Didn't you know that?"

"No," Mom replied. "He is now calling when Pia is already on the management track and insulting her. He must end it."

"You say that. I'll call Bill," replied Jölan.

"Yes, do that."

It was a victory for Mom and me. But it continued for three and a half years.

When Bill realized that he had nothing to do with it, he warned me of a teacher who was anti-Semitic. But I didn't tell anyone. Nor did I tell anyone that we were cousins. No one would know this. He stopped trading because there was too much anti-Semitism. I laughed roughly at him. You who have your Swedish appearance and Swedish surname, I thought.

Bill looked like a fisher from the west coast, pretty with a wide back and coarse hands. His face was bitter with a blunt nose and small eyes and greasy hair. His name was Gunnarsson after his father. He was simply mad. Jölan became a widow, and Bill died before his mother of AIDS, but the shame was too great for Jölan who gave money to the cancer fund instead. She was a very bitter woman who often argued and threw curses. She was in favor of her little sister and her children. She hated me because I wanted my cousin to go home for Christmas to celebrate with her parents as I had wedding management to take care of in 1983. A few years later, after I finished my studies, Bill was similar with his mother when it was chaotic. When he had run out on a woman, it was fitting to force his aunt and cousins rage. Then we did. He didn't want others to know that his mother was Jewish. He had been teased for this in Mölnlycke.

Jölan tried to insert a wedge between us siblings before she died in 2013, which was thirty years after the phone call described above, by telling us that we were welcome to come home to visit her and take what we wanted from her household. Jölan thought I influenced Bill's death by explaining to my fellow students that we were cousins. It happened about ten years after I had finished my studies. We siblings did not want to feel like ravens robbing something away. We also had no good contact with her because of her annoying and envious attitude. As you can see, Jölan was very ill in her perception, and it was unpleasant to be accused and cursed at by her. But she survived my mother. When she died neither me nor any of my siblings got any inheritance. She donated everything to the cancer fund. There was no sensible explanation as to why the money would be there when her son died of AIDS, but the shame was too great to donate money to AIDS.

That was the background with Bill and my aunt Jölan. Now I'll get back to my studies.

In 1978, I switched to a group with Bill's best friend's girlfriend. Now Bill was able to keep me cool for the rest of my studies. There was a couple who came from Arvika. They lived at Rådmansgatan, and we often gathered there. We ate at different vegetarian restaurants, and I was finally free of the greasy homecooked dishes in the yellow villa. That was nice. The girl came from the country and told me one night that when she had trouble sleeping she would take a walk.

Then she became angry and stagnated. A car drove up and wove down the road. The driver asked, "How much do you charge?"

She grinned and took nothing. "What do you mean?"

"How much do you charge for a lie?" asked the cod.

"What do you really mean?" she asked again.

"I can pay a lot, you should know," replied the cod.

Then she hurried home. The next day, she told us this. Then we continued to study, do group work, take exams, and work through the next three and a half years.

I finally got my bachelor apartment when I turned twenty years old. It was a cute little one on the currency road. From the dining room, there was a wonderful view of the treetops and Lake Mälaren. I had four stools for seating and a sitting bath in the bathroom with a window to vent out the misty air. The living room and bedroom were one room. Dad helped me buy a sofa bed and a bookshelf that I found in the room, and I could look out through the big windows that were there. Unfortunately, there was no balcony, but I was able to talk about myself and get a study.

I was able to invite over my fellow students and do the tasks in peace. It was a great relief. The rent was six hundred kronor a month, and I had enough to cover it with my student loans, study grants, and summer law work I earned to cope with the economy. I had to eat at home with my mother on Saturdays and had dinner by myself. We had some parties too.

I remember a Lucia party where we went out and mingled. It was a word that did not exist then. The girl from the country thought I was a little shy and needed to be more social. It might have been true because I was influenced by my Orthodox home environment. When I hung out at some parties, I ended up dancing with a man who pushed himself close to me and started to hang out. I was somewhat drunk. Not fully drunk but enough to not react fast enough. The girl thought it was good that I had found someone and left. Another guy came up to me. Suddenly, there were three of us, and I began to feel uncomfortable. They wanted us to continue somewhere else. Then a warning signal went off in my head. No, I did not want to. I felt cold and walked away. Fortunately, they released me. I remember that the white embroidered dress I had been wearing was stained with red wine. I don't remember how that happened.

I came home and slept off the hangover then felt cold over what I experienced the night before. I told the girl who just grinned. She chewed gum and looked stupid. I thought it was disrespectful. Okay, now I knew how she reacted. I lived by my values and respected others' values, but they did not respect mine. Then I understood where my boundaries were. I separated my study and leisure time. Leisure time I spent with my Jewish friends who respected me better.

Life After My Studies

Most of my relatives lived in America, and I thought I'd settle there and meet my dream prince. Instead, I found an American in the Golan Heights. When I finished my studies, I went on a long and much-needed journey to Israel. I visited relatives in Netanya, Haifa, and Jerusalem. Dad's cousins lived in the religious parts of the city. Nelly was a determined lady with a blond wig that she put on the hat shelf at night. I remember when I went up one night to empty my bladder and was frightened by the luminous blonde wig, not understanding what it was doing there.

Nelly had a plan for me. She wanted me to find a man to marry. One Friday night, she wanted me to go to the nearest synagogue by myself. I thought the atmosphere felt uncomfortable and grumpy. I was used to going to synagogue on Saturdays and big holidays. She insisted that I go, but I refused. I pointed out that my parents would not appreciate me going alone on a Friday night to a synagogue service. She let me be.

I had another plan. I booked a bus ticket to northern Israel and went to the Golan Heights. I just disappeared without saying anything to Nelly.

She wasn't happy with me because she had booked a date with a religious boy. I scoffed at her as if she were not wise. Why would she want me to marry a man who could not support himself? Her answer was that she supported her children and her husband. Her daughters worked as nurses, and she was a laboratory assistant.

I laughed at her and said, "Do you think I studied at the university to marry a man I would have to support?"

"Are you crazy?"

"Nelly, I am not."

"It is important to have a man and family."

It would have been a good idea to take me away with him. I went to another place, terribly annoyed that she put her nose in my business. My parents were also upset when I told them how she was treating me in Jerusalem. I took a tourist bus, still feeling upset about Nelly's actions, and talked to a nice American. His name was Jay, and he lived in New York. I thought he seemed much better than that shaking youngster who couldn't do anything but pray in the synagogue. I took over responsibility for myself.

My self-image was better after I completed my academic degree. I was someone who had a job and was able to support myself. No one would decide who I should marry and how my financial situation would be. Especially not a person I had never met before. We had a nice trip and watched *Star Wars*. We went our separate ways but exchanged addresses. I came home from my trip and started working and exchanging letters with Jay. It didn't happen much more.

One day Jay called when I was home with Mom.

Mom answered the phone. "Malvina."

"Hi, it's Jay…"

"Hi, Jay, are you gay?" she asked, and I thought it was really embarrassing.

I heard how Jay sharpened on the other end of the line and liked the situation.

I took the handset and apologized for Mom's jokes. Then it was out of the way, but I was ashamed at her childish reactions. I worked to move on, and so I went to the United States with my sister. My job was to marry an Orthodox in Brooklyn. It suited Jay who lived in Brooklyn and two of my friends I met the year before in Israel.

I remember when Jay came in with his Cadillac in 1981, and there was a rush of my mother's family. I landed in New York on Thursday with my sister and was already out on a date on Saturday night. My mother's uncle was quick. He said it was just as well that I was getting married. We could just have two weddings at the same time. I was terrified, and Jay was surprised.

He took me to his parents, and there we sat looking at photo albums. His parents anxiously asked if there was a high divorce rate in Sweden. They had heard that there was, but I told them that I didn't know. Jay was their only son, and the mother thought Jay and I could move into the upstairs until we had somewhere to live. I started to look red and had the series *Dallas* fresh in my mind with all the relatives who sneaked into each other's privacy and said that we do not live in Sweden.

My sister and I looked at each other. Jay was an authorized accountant and served well in Manhattan. He thought I could become his assistant. I wanted to read more about economics. He thought it was a waste of time and asked why I wanted to read about it. Before I could answer, he put on a country song with Dolly Parton and drove quickly to the Brooklyn Bridge. It just wouldn't work. We separated, and I said we were too different. I understood that I would not have much say if I married him.

I did not want to throw away the improved self-image I had developed after four years at the university or lose the feeling that I was good enough and become dependent on his good will. Become his assistant? No, I really didn't want to. I didn't even like business economics, and I didn't want to live at home with his parents, especially not his very curious mother. No thanks.

My sister and I went on to Pittsburgh where my dad had cousins. They had mixed feelings about our observations and the family's reactions.

One cousin told me that Milton believed Dad had died in the war. When they found out that he had survived the concentration camps, they believed that he would not be able to survive for a long time and could not have children. This was thrown straight into our faces. In spite of my twenty-three years, I understood what cold cousins he had. My sister understood that too, and we also understood why Dad didn't get his fair share after Grandma's death. The corps had taken care of that, Cousins. Dad told me that when he was over in America in 1969 he saw his mother's diamond ring on her aunt's hand. There were also other things they took from my father, who was more important. It was his self-image. They didn't want him. They just played a game of being friendly and didn't help him with his dream of coming over to America. My sister and I understood that they didn't want us there. They got the chance but didn't want poor Dad, who lived with his dream all his life and been betrayed by his mother and then his cousins, to have one.

My little sister and I thought it was good to see how they really were. We talked about this very clearly to Mom when we got home so she would hit Dad's grills out of his head. We also didn't think that Mom would cater to Dad's cousins by preparing three-course dinners when they came to visit us. Some visited us or sent distant relatives to visit.

We made our parents change their mind after that trip. Then we took the train past Philadelphia and stayed longer in Chicago, which we thought was the nicest part of the trip. The cousins living there were lawyers and judges, and I liked them better. My sister had the law in common with them as well. We stayed in the city center, and my sister wanted chocolate croissants for breakfast every day. She got it.

We also took a detour to Toronto in Canada to see another cousin. It was a nice city, and we took the opportunity to see some of Canada.

We were on our way to visit one of Mom's cousins in Beverly Hills, but she stopped us from coming. It also wasn't fun to visit a cousin of my mother who lived in Baltimore, but we went back to New York and attended a great wedding in Manhattan. There were flowers from floor to ceiling and beautiful decorations. Women and men danced separately. The only thing that unified them was lifting the bride and groom in chairs and holding a handkerchief. Because we were at an Orthodox wedding, only the honorary table had mixed seating. All the other men and women at the party sat alone.

My sister and I had never been to such a wedding. It was like traveling back to another time. The wedding could have taken place in Mukacevo where our mother grew up. Both Vera and I did not feel comfortable with the distorted Orthodox style, but we behaved decently. I definitely didn't want to be involved in anything like that when I got married.

Dana wore a wig and refused to be seen without it. She was not shaved under the wig. I suppose it was very hot to have her own hair under the wig in the summer. My sister and I did not understand the point and thought she should be shaved under the wig.

After the wedding, Jay and I went back to our lives. As things continued, I began to worry about not finding the right man to marry. My classmates from Hillelskolan were already married or engaged. I was about twenty-four years old. How would things turn out? I didn't want to be an old maid.

That spring there was a party at the Session Hall, and I planned to go with my brother, but then he wasn't allowed to go. I was brave and went myself. All the bachelors surrounded me, and I could pick and choose as they threw themselves around me as if I were a sugar cube. They weren't the men I wanted. They were the leftovers that no one wanted. I started to lose hope.

But then David came from nowhere and took me to a table. I was happy and sat down with him. David had lived for several years abroad. He first lived in Israel and later in the United States. It had been several years since I saw him. He was quite tall and slim and looked handsome. Perhaps he was somewhat withdrawn and a little pale but clearly looked better than the other men, and I thought he would change. Today, David looks like a frog ball. He now has a large abdomen that hangs above his narrow legs. He has a forehead like a great grapefruit, as Philip described it to me, and some straws on his head.

My hair was down and started burning when a candle lit it. He was alert enough to quickly extinguish the fire. I took that as a sign that he was alert enough to date me. Then we were up and running. We often met, and I became expectant.

He turned twenty-eight in the spring, and I baked a Schwarzwald cake. I roasted and chopped up hazelnuts, whisked the batter, baked the cake, and frosted it with whipped cream. I garnished the top with chocolate that I had melted and shaped in equally sized pieces. It impressed everyone.

We got engaged on a midsummer evening at Bergby, a small town north of Norrtälje. The house was dark brown, and I had it decorated with yellow buttercups. It was very romantic on the engagement. I wore a blue silk skirt and white lace blouse, and David wore a suit when he put the engagement ring on my finger. My parents looked happy. Even the in-laws and my siblings did. David's cousin was there with her fiancé out of courtesy. They looked more strained.

We were there on vacation. David and I went sunbathing and then swimming. We also took an Åland cruise. He kept me up when the sun went down, and it felt like I had gotten what I wanted. I was done with my education, had a permanent job, and now I would form a family. At last, I was catching up with life, I thought. I wanted to be like everyone else and was probably stressed about getting too old to get married. My mother often nagged that I had to have children before I was thirty years old. She was afraid that I would otherwise give birth to a sick child. If not for that, I would have taken it slower and waited to marry. I would have seen more of David's weaknesses if I waited.

After a while, I woke up to all of his failures. If I'd known ahead of time, it would have stopped me from having a family with him. But hindsight is twenty-twenty. I felt like I had gotten what I wanted then and was ready. At last, I was catching up with life.

Autumn came, and I started to feel pressure. Soon I would be twenty-five years old, as my mother constantly reminded me. I started grumbling and talking to David about his future plans. He worked with his father and traveled extensively abroad.

We talked a lot about how important it was to find a livelihood. David also wanted a family, but he might not have been as stressed about it as me. I had the pressure from my parents to succeed in getting into a nice family and having Jewish children. My biological clock ticked, and I was already trained with a permanent job. I had already worked for a couple of years, so it was okay to have children. My employers would not grumble. But David was not catching up.

He didn't set up a job with his dad. My father-in-law played an important role for me and my parents because we thought he had such good contacts. I wish my parents could have seen through the game. But they were stuck on the fact that I would finally get into a fine Orthodox family. It didn't grow on trees right away. My dad had great confidence that David's grandfather was just overbearing. The family must simply be good according to my dad's way of thinking.

I had feelings of guilt over my parents' horrible war experiences and wanted to make them happy. I had no idea what I was giving in to. I was misled like a blind cow in her booth about to be slaughtered. What would I choose? There was no one else in Stockholm. I had tried my luck abroad, but it was not for me. I had not lived for a long time abroad, but my education was adapted to Swedish conditions, so it would have been difficult to get a job abroad.

My mother's cousin offered to arrange an internship in the White House. But Dad advised me not to jump on it. I listened to him and have regretted it many times. But later in life, I had to meet a good friend of my mother's cousin who also worked in the White House. Maybe he was part of the planning if I had taken the internship? I was in a fox hole. If I had known what I know now, I would have drawn my ears and gotten out, but I wanted to make it work.

I assumed he was just a little shy, and I would help him become more outgoing. I didn't see the warning signs that he often sat for himself in a chair when the others mingled. He behaved oddly by having a few phrases that he repeated with everyone. When he was done, he just sat in a corner and stared blankly into space. He could disappear for no reason, leaving me to worry about what he was doing. His family did not want to say that David had severe communication problems or that he was not capable of forming a family.

It takes quite a lot for a man to take responsibility for another person and especially for a child. How could a young woman starting a family for the first time know that? It was hard. I was too naive to understand. Who could I compare him to? The interactions I had with the men in the congregation who were almost as snappy or quirky? In that world, he was like them. He was normal. But in the outside world, he was not normal. I should have been more alert and checked with others, but I just checked with his family, who obviously didn't want to tell us what was going on.

My parents were also fooled into thinking that everything was fine. Later, my dad had rubbed in that I had ended up in such a terrible situation. Yes, and what was I supposed to say? Maybe things would have been different if I had parents who were adult enough to see what was good for me and not force me into a situation that was for their satisfaction. But as I was embarrassed, I said nothing when my father made me feel guilty. He compromised my life instead of his own.

I should have noticed how strange David's mother behaved. When people came over, she asked me to use a calculator to count how many cups of tea and coffee she needed to brew. She trembled with fear at the thought of brewing too much coffee or tea. I didn't understand why it was so important. The staff had taken care of the rest. They hired staff to assist with cooking, cleaning, and table setting for parties. His mother just had to worry about making coffee and tea.

Johanna also behaved strangely. When David took something out of the fridge to eat, she took it from him and put it back. There were several things that were not normal in the family.

Johanna pulled my mother into the bedroom and showed her sexy lingerie. Mom did not know how to react but talked to Dad about her strange behavior. Johanna was the daughter of an Orthodox rabbi. Mom thought it was inappropriate behavior. I shared my mother's opinion and did not understand why Johanna called my mother into the bedroom to show her such things. What was she trying to say? He was bad in bed? Did she need to make use of that type of clothing to become desirable? Was it a hint for me to also buy such lingerie? Doing so did not fit in our circles.

With my experience and age, I understood that Johanna was a very unhappy woman who could not satisfy her husband. He ran after other women. She was searching for a way to show it. Kurt looked like the mafia boss where he sat in his armchair with gold-coated lion pockets, smoking cigars. He told funny anecdotes from his travels that were appreciated because they were so foreign to the sadness of everyday life. That said, I was used to everyone being more or less quirky in my ward, so he seemed normal.

He was very different from my dad, who was a reserved and silent man with strict rules for how things should be and with a strong sense of integrity. Dad never took a stance and made sure to fit in. He was always properly and neatly dressed in matching clothes with ironed shirts and matching ties. He did not smoke and did not tell hilarious anecdotes like Kurt. Dad discussed politics and philosophy that many failed to follow in the Jewish circle in the south. But he just did it at home and with guests who visited us who were interested or pretended to be knowledgeable on the subject.

David's cousin married, and we were invited to the Opera Rotundan. It was a great event with at least three hundred guests. Carina came in a meringue wedding dress and was very made-up. They had known each other well before they got married and had lived together for seven years. I didn't understand why it would be such a fuss to them. But it was for appearances and to impress their grandfather. I felt a bit out of place because none of the guests were my friends and some were so horrible. I started to get hungry to marry, and we set a date for our wedding on the 13th of January 1983.

I remember how nervous I was when we had come out with the fact that we were getting married in the fall. Some already knew. Others thought it was time. Anyway, I was fully up to planning our wedding. I planned out how people would sit. I decided the color theme—white and blue, the colors of the Israeli flag. The Israeli embassy and the trade attaché were invited. Mom took me to NK where I chose a lace dress reminiscent of Princess Diana's wedding dress. Mine was a simpler variant, and I chose a suitable veil with a diadem at a special store that Carina recommended to me. Then there were the flowers. David didn't understand how important it   was. I chose a drop shape with white flowers reminiscent of Princess Diana's bridal bouquet. I thought it would sparkle next to my black-haired hair, and it did. I was an ice princess. Shoes. Where did I find white shoes in January? It was only ten degrees outside, but I decided on my Chantal sandals in white and gold.

There were no wedding fixers at that time. It was the closest family members who fixed the parties. However, one of my friends helped me by having her friends from the Music Academy play music. Her fiancé was a party photographer, and we had a special bride photographer. The guests took a chartered bus from the Session room where the wedding was to the Stallmästaregården. We had three men who betrothed us. David's grandfather Emil, who was the chief rabbi of Bologna, assisted the Orthodox rabbi Smalts, and the cantor was Dov Feinstein. We had been training for a long time to do Mendelssohn's "Wedding March." My mother-in-law's blue hat shook with nervousness, and Mom laughed when she saw this because she was nervous too. Everyone was.

David came in first with his father and mother. They were followed by my sister and his sister, who had come as bridesmaids. Then I came in with my mother and father. David's grandfather read prayers for forty-five minutes. It felt like an eternity. Finally, I walked seven laps around David, and the others congratulated us as he broke a glass as usual.

My colleagues had attended the wedding ceremony along with other acquaintances. The guests were bused to Stallmästaregården, and there the whole family was photographed in front of a beautiful tapestry. We sat at a beautifully set table with white damask cloth, pink roses, gold light boxes, and crystal dishes with gold details. We ate an exquisite menu and were entertained by my friends with Mexican music and Gunilla's special songs.

It was a wonderful celebration that lasted longer than our marriage. I felt lucky to have come so far. I was educated and had permanent employment working full time in my area of expertise. Now I was going to make a family with my husband, who was accepted by my family. His dad would help him succeed in his business. It wouldn't be that hard, I thought, with Kurt's contacts. How wrong I was.

We moved into my small apartment in Valutavägen and took a short trip to Oslo for a quick honeymoon. I would call it a honeymoon. Anyway, we had planned to do it later when it got warmer. We went to the French Riviera early in the summer.

But shortly after the Germany trip, David went to the United States and was away for two months. He went without telling me ahead of time. At first, I was shocked then I was sad. I knew he was going to travel, but I thought he would tell me ahead of time. He just left and called from Germany to tell me that he would be away for a long time in America.

Johanna told me that he lived with his old girlfriend, and it hit my heart when she told me. My dad thought I should leave David for behaving like that, but I was emotionally bound to him and wanted to give him more chances. David had lived abroad for several years after high school. His father would help him for a year while he got on his feet in Sweden, so I could feel financially secure. Then David would manage himself with all the contacts he had made. We had moved into an apartment on Svanbacken because I changed my one at the housing office.

We bought the most necessary furniture, and I had a dowry with towels, cutlery, and crockery for the nest. David came with empty pockets, which I thought was strange. His parents were rich. I had no idea. My parents didn't at first either. So, it continued. We met in Nice and had it cozy. We went around to the nice resorts of Antibes, Monaco and relaxed. Then I had to get back to work, and David returned to traveling.

We never argued, but my questions were perceived as quarrels. David fled from me throughout our marriage. He was a scared little hare. I didn't understand that he had serious communication problems.

I hoped everything would work out. I felt happy about having a little baby in me and thought everything would settle. That confidence waivered within a month when the jewelry shop at Fridhemsplan that David worked in was robbed, and he closed it again. I had come by to check on him to see if he wanted to go for lunch, and there he stood with his tail between his legs. "I was robbed," he said. "There is nothing left in the store."

When I Was Expecting a Child

It was New Year's Eve, and I thought it might be better if we had a baby. I got pregnant and hoped that David would pull himself together if he had a child to take responsibility for. When I tried to talk to David about various vital things like his job and travel, he disappeared. We never argued, but David couldn't handle my questions. He escaped from me throughout our marriage. He was terrified and worried. I thought maybe he knew what he was doing when he tricked me. At the time, I didn't understand that David had serious communication problems.

It didn't work either. I became depressed and desperate. It was January 1984, and now I was expecting a child, and there was no return. Why didn't he get his act together? I had bought him perfectly matched clothes so he would look decent. It didn't help.

David could not sell to customers. What could he do? It was too late to do something now. I was pregnant and would soon be a mother. In March, the goldsmith's business was robbed, and David had to stop working there.

"Sharpen, David. You're going to become a father soon, and you must be able to contribute to our family's livelihood. I can't do everything," I said to David.

I became a little nauseous the first time, but I went to work as usual. I felt happy about having a little cute baby in me. I had seen Philip's body in an ultrasound, and it was real. I imagined him as being very sweet with blue eyes and light brown hair. He has the exact look I believed he would before his birth.

I was extra hungry for oranges and worked out. I felt a growing concern for David's shortcomings, but I had confidence that he was getting ready. His last attempt at a business was selling authentic oriental pearls, but that business ran out of steam just before Philip was born.

I came to realize that David had Asperger's syndrome. He did not recognize that, but it became apparent during a diagnosis of my son several years later.

We were going to practice breathing together. David didn't come all the time, and I complained loudly to my mother-in-law. I was afraid to give birth. Mom had told me that I waited a day to be born at Södersjukhuset. If you have a difficult birth into the world then it sets up how you're received by the world during life. In my case, I think that is true, unfortunately.

Mom told me that there were Lucia in white dresses singing and bidding on lussebullar. She told me that she always wanted the room's window opened to air out the smell in the room, but the other patients froze and didn't like the weather. With this fresh in my memory, I prepared myself. Mom came with all her strength, and quite rightly I had the whole room filled with doctors. A nurse pulled over all the carts she could. There was a risk that I would need to have a cesarean section.

Seven hours later, I was given pelvic floor anesthesia and nitrous oxide. They cut into my abdomen to get Philip out. Like me, he had the umbilical cord around his neck. The doctors quickly removed it, and he was put in the incubator. The birth had gone well, but he needed extra warmth while I got over twenty stitches.

During the birth, they offered me a mirror so that I could see, which I declined. Despite that, Mom replied for me that we wanted a mirror, but the doctors knew I didn't, and I threw her out of the room. I saw the whole birth through the glass window's reflection in the early hours of the 11th of October 1984.

David spent most of his time sleeping in a chair. Mom managed to wake him up when Philip was born. Then he fell back asleep. It was typically David. I set my baby on my stomach for a while, and he was really sweet.

I was newly redeemed and told about the time thereafter.

I stayed at Karolinska Hospital for four days, learning to change diapers and trying to breastfeed. David also learned some things but was not participating. Once, I was not fast enough changing a diaper, and Philip peed a ray straight into my face. The little golden king didn't know what he was doing. Then I realized that I needed a special technique to change the diaper on my little guy. On the fifth day, we went home, and my mother wanted to come along, but I'd had enough of her help. Unfortunately, she was hurt that I didn't want her there, but I wanted peace and quiet.

Once we were home, I continued to try to get started on breastfeeding. It was difficult as a first-time mother to start breastfeeding. In the hospital, midwives struggled, clumsily pulling my nipples as if I were a cow that would milk on request. There was no fine sensitivity there. They tested various aids but none work. In the end, breastfeeding started at home when Philip and I got a quiet moment. He was so ravenous that he got a stomachache.

Long into the small hours, I had to keep him over my shoulder to get him to sleep. I took walks with Philip in the stroller, and David was ashamed to walk near us. I do not know if it was because he did not want to show that he was a father or if he was embarrassed that the baby carriage was not the most expensive one that could be bought. David had major problems connecting to Philip. He refused to change his diaper, and the few times he did it were accompanied by great protests.

He would sometimes walk around with Philip, and once I caught him dripping gruel on his nipple to try to get Philip to breastfeed. I don't know why he did this. Was he jealous of the contact I had with Philip? Or was it his mother who gave such advice as a new psychologist at the age of sixty? Mom and Dad often visited me when I was on parental leave and worried about David's behavior.

A few months later, I was twenty-seven years old, and David became increasingly absorbed in his depression. He had nightmares and scared me. His deal to sell oriental beads with his father failed, and he did not know how to make a living. I was on parental leave and had my hands full with Philip. David became increasingly apathetic. It seemed like he didn't want to be a dad.

I was busy coping with parenting every day but became more concerned about his behavior. I had hoped the baby would make him happy and give him something to live for. It had the opposite effect. Little had I imagined that he was totally unfit. That realization came stealthily every day. David slept as usual. I made him help every other night trying to get more sleep, but he didn't care for it.

Within our traditions, the mother's wishes on names are given priority. I wanted the boy to be called Philip. They decided that he would be given Grandpa's Hebrew name. I poked in Zvi, which means deer. When people congratulated us, it became embarrassing. Congratulations Philip or congratulations to Carl-Philip. It was Kurt who was a patriot and wanted Philip to be named after the crown prince.

Mom told me that a boy almost bled when he was circumcised. He was a man of my age. I comforted myself with the fact that now there was a surgeon.

On the eighth day, Philip was circumcised according to our traditions by a surgeon at home where we had a small party with the family. I had terrible anxiety around my son being circumcised. I was worried it would traumatize him, but I was under such great pressure, and I would be excluded unless my boy continued with the rituals our people had practiced for millennia. I selected a good surgeon from Gothenburg who was also educated in the religious rites of the ritual.

I thought my heart would jump out of my throat when Philip screamed his heartbreaking cry. I thought I was being cruel as a mother, but it would be even crueler if we were excluded from the Jewish. Many then followed the practice of having a surgeon conduct the ritual. It went well, and I checked Philip into the child care center.

After a month, it was time for pidyon, a party for first-born boys. It is traditional to invite a rabbi home and give him a fine meal to be formally accepted as a parent. I selected the finest pieces of meat for a pot, and we had a party. Rabbi Smalts would get money because I would symbolically get back my son. It is a tradition that the first-born boy is owned by the rabbi until the pidyon haben. I took great care to pay, and the rite was completed. It's an old custom, and I have never understood why it is still practiced, but when we were desert people and nomads, it surely filled a function.

So now I think David thought about what he did thirty years ago. He ruined my and my son's lives, no matter why he did what he did. The others who testified falsely before the wedding were subordinates. Among other things, his parents and his uncle had known David's difficulties since his childhood, but they withheld that information from me. No one said anything about the obstruction. Everyone knew he had issues and could have objected to the marriage to prevent the disaster. They chose to remain silent.

David's uncle was a parish chairman with great responsibilities. They wanted to get rid of the problem and off-loaded him on my young inexperienced shoulders. They also lied to my parents. David's grandfather spoke warmly about his grandchild. I still do not know if he had lied about David to keep the facade up or if he pretended not to know. He was also unintentionally responsible for David's lifelong disability, which is a genetic condition. In addition, a cantor who witnessed at the wedding was also involved in the silence.

Three were responsible for not breaking the silence before the wedding. Everyone was greedy for various reasons. Rabbi Smalts wanted money. David's grandfather wanted to see his grandson married and have a normal life. The office wanted to keep up with the Patsch family for various private reasons. I was caught in a stall like a cow being prepared for slaughter. And my dad complained bitterly after my divorce when he realized how groundless I had become.

So, it continued. I was split and had been swallowed by the delusion that David would make good money. I really needed his contribution to the household. The rent was high, and I didn't earn enough to cope with everything. I was employed as an officer in the municipality. Once, he traveled to Israel and tried to sell swimsuits. When he got home, he was completely finished. David told us the customs had taken all the swimsuits.

I was furious. "You can't handle anything," I told David.

David watched with puppy eyes, and I felt sorry for him, so I gave him several chances.

"How is it going to be?" I often asked David.

He shrugged his shoulders and said he was getting ready. In-laws thought they could go to Canada and try making money in natural gas. You yourself hear how he swung from one industry to another.

I started my descent into the Inanna myth and had lost my crown when I saw David not behaving like a dad. He was not fond of his first-born son. It hurt me a lot. It is a great thing to have a first-born son in our faith. His grandfather was overbearing, and Philip was his first boy grandchild. I had expected support but got the opposite. What was wrong with David? What didn't I know?

The next descent was when I had to take off my clothes like Inanna when I realized that I had to take complete responsibility for myself. David was not on my side. The last thing I took off was the lapis, according to the Inanna myth, and that was when I found David with empty eyes above a dropoff. It looked like he would at any time drop the stroller off the cliff. This was the morning of the 31st of December 1984. The moment is frozen in my memory.

It was a cold morning, and I needed to buy milk. I took Philip in the cart to the store, and David came along. We did a little walk together then I left Philip with David. When I got out of the store, David was not there. I did not have a cell phone to call in 1984. There were none then. I was really stressed out. Where could he be?

The minutes I ran around like a dizzy hen looking for Philip were awful. My panic increased with every passing minute. Where could David go with the pram? He was supposed to wait outside the store. David was depressed. Why did I leave him with the baby? Why didn't I let David buy milk instead? I blamed myself as I ran home and checked to see if he was there. No, he wasn't there. I ran back to the store and asked if anyone had seen them.

No, he was not there. I ran to a lookout point where there was a dropoff and hoped he was not there, but he was. He held the pram over the cliff's edge. His eyes were empty. He wanted to kill our son. Why? What was wrong with David?

I tore the stroller from his grip and ran home to call the police. When they arrived, I explained the situation and that David was deeply depressed. They wrote a report.

I called my sister who was home with my parents. She came at once and helped me pack up the essentials. I remember how I put on my boots, and David crouched to take them off again, trying to stop me from going. Vera took my things to Philip then pulled David aside.

Vera said, "Leave Pia alone."

"We need to get out of here now."

David asked me to tear up the police report. I did it out of mercy for him, and I regretted that later during a trial for the right of access a few years later. I was in shock. My sister took the pram, where Philip lay oblivious, and grabbed my arm. We headed towards the metro in Tallkrogen and went to the Gubbängen station to go home to my parents

Once at home, I broke down with Mom and cried. I couldn't say a word. Vera spoke for me, and Mom and Dad comforted me. I sat at the kitchen table, and my mother brought me a cup of tea and a sandwich. I ate the sandwich rudely and sipped the warming tea, which also calmed me.

David drove to Mom and Dad's house in his red Fiat and waited patiently for me and my baby to come home. He sat in the car for several hours, but he had to drive home alone.

Philip and I stayed overnight, and I had no idea how to continue with life. I just needed to be taken care of in a loving environment with Mom and Dad. After a day, I understood that I couldn't go home anymore. I had no idea what I was going to do. I couldn't continue to live under such stress. David did not remember his outbursts. He was in such poor condition that he could not judge what was good for our son. He was dangerous.

The days went by and became weeks. Philip and I stayed with my parents for a couple of months. Life went on.

I remember when Dad followed me home to Svanbacken to pick up diapers for Phillip and clothes for both of us. David sat in his office smoking with his sister. They did not greet us and stared at us as if we were strangers. They didn't ask how I felt or how Philip was doing. They just sat there planning to take everything that was of value.

Another time, they had snatched up all the things and thrown them into a pile because David planned to take everything. I contacted a lawyer to find out how the whole thing would be resolved. Kurt had already gone to Silbersky, so David already had a representative.

I lived at Mom and Dad's home, and I remember when Kurt called Mom thinking we could change the four-room in Svanbacken to two one-room apartments. Mom got hysterical and said, "Are you an idiot, Kurt?"

"It is enough for each of them."

Mom answered furiously, "You can arrange an apartment for your son."

"It was Pia who moved him to the apartment they are living in."

"David came with two empty pockets."

"You promised they would move into an apartment in the middle of the city."

Mom slammed the phone in the old man's ear.

After a couple of days, I was told that David was being assisted by Silbersky's lawyers after my father-in-law had advised him to pay the high attorney fees. It was a circus. What was I supposed to do? I couldn't defend myself against Silbersky. I got a tip to hire a female lawyer, Billner.

I knew something was wrong a short while before the breakup and had written down down a list of my belongings and asked David to sign the paper. I brought it to Billner who said it was too sloppy for her to help me but that I could try to use it as a marriage contract myself. I got through it at the district court. It was the first victory. But I could not afford to pay the rent, as my entire income would have to go to it. David would have access rights.

If I refused him, he could get custody even though he didn't want it He didn't care about my son. For him, it was about prestige, to show others that he was normal. He wanted to show me what he was capable of doing. His mother was a newly graduated psychologist and provided him with various psychological behavior profiles to attempt to crack me. All of this woman's screws were loose.

I called his grandfather and super-rabbi, Emil, to ask why David couldn't get a decent job. His answer was, "David works with Kurt."

"No, he doesn't."

"He has tried several industries."

"It just makes a mess of everything."

"It was not my intention that I would manage everything."

"Kurt guaranteed that David would be on his feet within a year with his fine contacts."

"He lied and knew about it,"

"What are you telling me?" I asked.

Emil took so badly that he had a heart attack, I later learned. David's cousin Carina called me to tell me it was my fault. I realized that I had been cheated in a conspiracy like the worst Borgian family in Italy.

I tried to find a solution to the situation. One day I saw a small note in Konsum about an apartment change. A third in Tulevägen was replaced by an apartment in Svanbacken. I looked at the apartment that was next to my mom's house. But the apartment was rundown. In the hall, there were wine-red brothel tapestries and large holes in the walls. The living room wallpaper was olive and pea-green. In the kitchen, there was brown and fire-yellow wallpaper and matching kitchen cupboards. It was disgusting. All child-resistant contacts were broken. I do not understand how a family of children could live that way.

I contacted the host who assured me that the apartment would be refurbished before I moved in. They did the renovations, but it took a long time to get everything in order. They had to arrange cleaning help. After all, I had left a brand new apartment without a scratch that was closer to the city and had a nice lake view. After many trips, I got the apartment because the baby needed good accommodations.

Moving with My Baby

We moved in April 1985 after having lived with Mom and Dad since New Year's Eve. Dad helped me move. I nursed Philip and pumped out the milk so Mom could feed him. There was no one else who helped me. I felt so lonely. As the days went by, I cared for Philip and walked. I don't remember getting any support from friends during the break. They thought it was too hard to talk about. Where were my friends? Where were my siblings?

My brother said, "As you sleep, you lie down." It was absolutely heartless. He more than anyone had gotten a lot of support with borrowing money for all his car parts and accessories. I had always arranged everything myself. When I needed help, it was unusual.

I had to move to a cheaper apartment. I got my life and finances in order quickly. I was lucky that I could find an apartment near my parents and that it was possible to exchange it with the apartment in Svanberg. David had no involvement. On the contrary, his father had called and complained to my mother. Kurt had the guts to call and ask that my apartment be replaced by two different ones. I had moved from my apartment to the apartment in Svanberg. David came empty-handed, and then Kurt wanted David to get something out of this even though I nursed the baby and needed peace and quiet. Where was Kurt's money? He promised to help us get an apartment in the city. It was just empty promises.

A colleague of mine wanted to sell his apartment in the city to me, but I did not take the opportunity. It was not fair, and I was careful that everything went properly. In addition, the apartment was only a few blocks from my in-laws. They would never let David go from such a treasure, and Johanna would be there all the time. At the separation, I was grateful that I at least let that go. Later, I felt that I could easily switch to something else. But everything has its price.

I had to prepare for the trial against David, and it took all my strength. Kurt was a ferret who did everything to take advantage of me. Heartlessly, he came up with one duping proposal after another for David. David made a claim for deductions for dry cleaning to avoid maintenance. Johanna hooked on. They behaved like the worst mafia parents. I saw nothing Jewish in their behavior, nothing that suggested Johanna had a Jewish upbringing with a rabbi as a father. The greed and revenge took over everything in the name of defending their honor. Their son would be cleared at any price. Neither I nor my child was important compared to their reputation.

The price to live in the city then would be too high. After six months of separation, it was time for the trial and a divorce.

My sister joined me at the trial and followed it all. She was not a lawyer then but gave me advice. My lawyer didn't help much for the money she received from me. Most of the things I had to arrange myself, including several meetings with the authorities. I remember when my lawyer just sat down for a meeting, and I brought my own action. When the meeting was finished, she gave me a pat on the shoulder and said I had done well. My thought was, But why were you here? Though I didn't dare say that to my lawyer.

I got many questions from her like why did I marry a man like him? She did not understand my cultural background and how the second generation was the link to healing for their parents. The lawyer could have done much better. Instead, she gave me feelings of guilt that would take years to work away with therapists. Those who sat in the trial did not know about Asperger's syndrome and empathy disorders. They could not judge fairly in the case. I had to live with deep anxiety that David could kill Philip every time he met him.

I didn't want David to hang out with the baby. He wanted to kill our son, but it was very difficult to remove him from Phillip's life altogether. The visits had to be with someone who checked that everything went right. What was wrong with David? I tore the stroller from him and ran home to call the police, I told the district court. David came home, and two police officers sat there asking what had happened. I told the court that the police made a report to the district court at the trial where David's right of access was tried.

We were both responsible for arranging friends to be there every two weeks for a few hours when David met his son. David had no friends, so I had to arrange it with Alma. David did not always come at the assigned times, but everything still fell on me. Alma did not understand how David could be so mean. She was fifteen years older than me and had been married to a Moroccan man who was also nasty. I remember how Alma could feel after being subjected to David's energy. She said he was very negative and evil. Alma went through a spiritual development that I had to take part in. If Alma hadn't been there with Philip the times David came then I don't know what would have happened.

David felt very bad. If the courts had known more about different diagnoses, then they would have prevented David from exposing us to what he did. But thirty years ago, they couldn't do anything about such mental pressure and knew little about what it was.

Once, he came with a bearded bachelor who would witness David. Yes, everything seemed to be in order. As if he could do something about it. It was Kurt's friend. He drank alcohol with a colleague who David arranged as a check. I protested because he was inappropriate. This went on for two years.

The Jewish families did not understand that all this happened to me. They were duped by the family's generous contributions to Jewish charities and private parties. The greed defeated justice in those who considered themselves to be Orthodox. My family saw what money can do to people. They obviously came to the synagogue on Saturdays and prayed as usual, believing that they were fair people and used abuse, money, and other things to defend the facade. Anyone who had received bribes such as mink furs, goods, or other services was loyal to the corrupted family I was in.

Today, they have weakened, and people dare say what they think. It has taken almost thirty years for the Jewish community to confess the truth. People then believed that they were still rich and wanted to frolic in that lifestyle. Very true, I was invited to the shows at parties with waitresses serving fine food and drinks and expensive works of art on the walls to arouse reputation.

Money gives power. It is also so with religious people, maybe even more so. Where is the goodness?

I started working again after the parental leave ended, and my mother took Philip for the first year. She didn't want Philip to go to daycare as a baby, and I was grateful for that. I was off on the weekends, and Mom didn't have him then. When I got a couple of hours off every two weeks, I went to see Kia's classmate from high school. I got a massage and relaxed with a cup of tea. Kia then lived in a one-room apartment in Bandhagen. She was free as a bird, and I went through a separation and two divorces with a small child. Those moments gave me the strength to fight further.

I was greeted by her popular black cat in the hall. Often, he bit me in the big toe, but Kia snatched him away. Then that lovely moment with a cup of tea and where she told me what was happening to David. Kia looked around and said she did not understand how he could be so mean. She met various men she was not so fond of, but none of them had behaved as badly as David. I was jealous of her not having to feel the same pressure to marry as I did. She also didn't have to be in my dilemma. I think she also felt great gratitude for not having to go through what I did.

Finalizing My Divorce

I was finally divorced according to Swedish law and had again started working at the street office. Routines began to become more normal. Philip was nine months old. I nursed him, and he didn't want to be turned away. I continued until he was sixteen months old. In the end, he had to give up, but he didn't sleep well at night with a stomach ache. He only slept a few hours at night, and I was forced to work the next day. It was very hard. But I struggled through it.

I remember when I had bloated breasts at work, and my milk started to flow, making clear spots on my blouse. When I got home, I heard a little whining from upstairs. Philip would be nursing. That calmed him down, and when he was two years old, he cried helplessly every morning when I had to leave him. He wanted to be with Mom.

Philip was at home often because he was frequently sick with various infections. When Philip was two, I got hold of a day mother named Olga. She came from Portugal, and she worked with some children at home. Philip was the youngest. It was better than him being in childcare, I thought, because he was only two years old. I felt relief that someone else suited Philip, and he didn't have to depend on Mom.

I was home to care for him often but couldn't be home all the time. Aside from Olga, there were some aunts who were kind and played with Philip, and so it continued. Grandma checked how Philip was with the day mother and complained a lot that he didn't get along as well with her.

I needed to wait three years to get a Jewish divorce. David wanted to give up because I got away from him. He did everything to destroy my son and me. He was a real pig. He was helped by both his father and mother as he tried to keep up the image of being a suitable husband and father at all costs. It meant he told lies in the city about me. I realized that I was a subject of gossip with the devil and his family. Inanna was hung on a hook and rotted in the cave. That was how I felt. I wanted at all costs to come out of the cave but kept being pulled back down by new gossip David started.

David's uncle was chairman of the Jewish congregation and helped keep the radiance of their family intact. They destroyed our reputation, so it was difficult for my family and me to feel comfortable in the synagogue. Another rabbi told us about Smalts getting money to try to separate me. He received bribes from others. Fortunately, a classmate lived in Israel. Sanna was married to a man who was trusted by the rabbinate. He came to Sweden at regular intervals and checked that the Torah rolls were intact. Only some men are entrusted with the sacred work. Bengt was one of them.

Bengt also wrote a letter to the rabbinate where he described how they were failing David. He described his shortcomings as a father and husband in Hebrew.

It would not be accepted if, as a woman, I contacted the rabbi directly to ask them to help me. A woman cannot write to the rabbi herself. Only a righteous person who is accepted by the rabbi can represent her. It is very patriarchal, and it is the men who give their approval for a divorce. A woman is not entitled to demand one. She must prove that her husband did not fulfill her obligations under Jewish law.

What would I have done if I didn't have Bengt? After three difficult years, a man came to Stockholm and checked how the religious took care of the city. He found large gaps and shortly thereafter another man came who gave couples divorces. There were perhaps ten families who were freed from their shackles.

My dad wept for happiness that I would be free from these horrible people. He often said, "What have you done to be treated like this?" Dad felt great guilt about being deceived. He did not understand how it happened. He did not understand how the daughter of a rabbi could be such a devil. It was outside his frame of reference.

Dad said, "Now you're free to marry a decent man."

I answered, "I'm not ready to marry. I have a small child to take care of, and I have not had time to recover from stigmatization."

"Yes, now that you are divorced, you have the right to meet others and find someone who is suitable," Dad said.

He was very conservative and strict over my decency. It affected him and his position. If his daughter was a slut, it would ruin the whole family's reputation. He worried about my siblings and their chances of finding suitable spouses. What Dad did not understand was that there were no suitable candidates at all for my siblings. The other parents tried to get their children to stay abroad for long periods in order to establish links with future families and partners. Dad didn't. Poor Father tried to help the whole family, but he had difficulty prioritizing his immediate family. If we'd had the opportunity to go to Israel immediately after high school as everyone else had, our choices would have been far better. The probability of finding someone there was much greater than at home in Stockholm. But Dad was afraid violence would explode in the streets and that we would die in Israel.

Dad's war experiences were so strong that he could not distinguish between different things. He had children for that. I remember when they called home and asked my dad to let me go to Israel after high school. They threatened him by saying that it was a sin to not allow his children to do so. But Dad played the victim. It was too hard for him with his war experiences. He did not manage to think about it from my perspective. So, I studied at the university instead and married an inappropriate person because of the intense pressure I had from home.

There had been no chance for me to break this unwritten law. Being with a non-Jew would not have been tolerated. I was threatened with being declared dead. It's about the same thing as honor killings that Arab girls face. The difference is that I would not be physically killed but mentally killed. I would not belong to my biological family or have any rights.

I gave in and tried to do my best. Therefore, my father had severe guilt when my marriage went so wrong. Dad was so happy that he got to take me to the altar for a Jewish Orthodox wedding. I was the only child, and he felt proud of that point. At least he got me to go to the altar. I was his pride and joy.

When my son grew up, we had other difficulties in life, so I didn't often attend synagogue. That was part of why my son was not accepted into the synagogue. He disturbed the scheme with his autistic way. I felt hurt and went to synagogue only when my mother and sister were with me as a shield. For a long period of time, this kept me outside of the synagogue, and he did not get his Bar Mitzvah. I walked away from the congregation and felt betrayed. When Mom was buried by a Chassidic rabbi in 2005, the spark came back, urging me to search for my roots again. Now I go to synagogue more often.